Under the Rainbow

By

Dr. Lydia A. Woods

Channing & Watt Publishers
Peoria, AZ

Under the Rainbow, Copyright © 2020 Dr. Lydia A. Woods

All poems in this book were previously published and copyrighted by Dr. Lydia A. Woods.

All rights reserved.

Channing & Watt Publishers
Peoria, Arizona
www.channingandwatt.com

For information contact:
info@channingandwatt.com

Front Cover Photo /Book Design by
JD Woods Consulting

Back Cover Photo by
William C. Terry

No part of this publication may be reproduced, stored in a retrieval system, copied in any form or by any means, electronic, mechanical, photocopying, recording or otherwise transmitted without written permission from the publisher. You must not circulate this book in any format without permission in writing from the author or publisher. For permissions, contact Channing & Watt Publishers at: info@channingandwatt.com

First Edition

Printed in the United States of America

ISBN: 978-1-941200-07-0

Other Publications by Dr. Lydia A. Woods

Poems by Revelation
For the Edification of the Saints
Food for Saints
Let Those With Ears…
Conversations with the Saints
All the Saints Agree
Acceptance with Joy
Those Bible Women
Those Bible Characters
The Joy of the Lord
Made in the Fire

Dedicated to

My Granddaughters
Ayla, Adia, Kheper-ut, Hui-Shu-Byi

Acknowledgements

I want to give special thanks to my sister for her cover design and many hours of formatting for publication. Her unique skills and talents are invaluable to me!

Thank you, Holy Spirit, for using my humble vessel and letting me put my name on these words.

Introduction

Under the inspiration of the Holy Spirit, I began writing Christian poetry. When I look back at the beginning, I realize now that I knew very little about the Holy Spirit and His relationship to me. At first, I would be awakened during the night, out of a sound sleep, with a poem forming in my head, or sometimes while driving, or in the midst of conversation with someone.

I would tell people that the Spirit would come and go, then months later return, to give me poems. My understanding has since grown, and I now know that the Spirit never leaves and is always present with me and in me and thru me – the two of us are one.

I believe the Holy Spirit, is God and that God exists in every human being. The real gift of life is discovering God within you, which first blesses you, then those around you.

These collections of poems are inspired by the lessons which the Lord has been teaching me as I walk with Him. Many poems are inspired by uplifting and stimulating conversations with God's precious Saints and others, are born out of the frustration that many do not know the love of God and His amazing grace and mercy.

In reading, I hope you will find poems that speak to your heart, express what you have experienced, or have enlightened your understanding. The writing of these poems allows me an outlet of spiritual expression, as the Lord tempers and prepares me for my calling.

In 2009, while pursuing the Master of Divinity and the Master of Christian Education degrees at the Interdenominational Theological Center (ITC) in Atlanta, Georgia, I wrote a Master's thesis entitled <u>Using Christian Poetry as a Pedagogical Tool in Christian Education</u>. In addition to writing the thesis, I also did a compilation of Christian poems for youth and young adults. That book was entitled *Under the Rainbow*.

As a student of biblical numerology, I wanted to use the symbolism of the number seven. Seven denotes completeness and spiritual perfection and is the most sacred number to the Hebrews. The whole Word of God is founded upon the number seven. This number is used more than all other numbers in the Word of God, except the number one.

So, I conceived of seven chapters with seven poems in each chapter. I wanted to address seven topics that might interest youth and young adults: The Father, Son and Holy Spirit; Finding Out Who You Are; Encouragement; Words of Advice; Fighting the Enemy; Those Bible People; and The Movies: Their Spiritual Messages. I hope this book can be a used as a tool for young people in the Christian education process.

Table of Contents

Poems

Chapter 1 - The Father, Son, and Holy Spirit
Ain't He All That! 1
He's Good At 2
Master of Masters 3
Pieces of Myself 5
Somethin' Told Me 7
That Small Still Voice 9
With His Own Blood 11

Chapter 2 - Finding Out Who You Are
A Bible Character 15
The Brightest Light 17
If Thou Be 19
I'm Not Lucky – I'm Blessed 21
It is Your Destiny 22
Scariest Journey 23
Simply Because You Are Mine 25

Chapter 3 – Encouragement
Be Not Afraid, Only Believe 29
Be Still! 30
Good News 31
Happy is the Woman or Man 33
Hero in You 34
It's Alright 35
Your Gifts and Talents 36

Chapter 4 – Words of Advice
Back Talk 39
Doin' the Israelite 41
Forgive or Forgive Not 44
Garbage in Garbage Out! 45
If You Want To Make God Laugh! 47
Lean Not 49

   Love is An Action 50
Chapter 5 – Fighting the Enemy
   But for Your Praying Saints 53
   Idols, Idols, Idols 55
   It's War! 57
   Just Do It! 59
   The Perfect Murder 61
   Put it All On! 63
   What's His Face? 65

Chapter 6 – Those Bible People
   Follow the Anointing 69
   Here I Am 71
   Highly Favored 73
   Joseph 75
   Just Said No 79
   She Was First 81
   So Be Like Job 83

Chapter 7 – The Movies: Their Spiritual Messages
   The Circle of Life 87
   E.T. 89
   If You Build It 91
   May the Force… 93
   The Mummy's Curse 94
   The Red Pill or the Blue 95
   The Richest Man in Town 97

Scriptural References
Chapter 1 - The Father, Son, and Holy Spirit
   Ain't He All That! 102
      Hebrews 1:2-3; John 1:1-5; Revelation 22:13 (KJV)
   He's Good At 103
      Genesis 1:3, 9, 12, 16, 24, 27, 31; Isaiah 14:27, 46:9-11 (KJV)
   Master of Masters 105
      Matthew 4:1, 4:19, 5:1, 7:29, 8:26, 11:5; Luke 8:43-48; John 2:1-11, 11:43-44 (KJV)
   Pieces of Myself 108

Hebrews 13:5; Romans 12:3; Ephesians 4:7 (KJV)
Somethin' Told Me 109
John 12:26; Ephesians 4:30; Luke 2:26 (KJV)
That Small Still Voice 110
Psalms 95:7; Hebrews 3:7 (KJV)
With His Own Blood 111
Acts 20:28; Hosea 2:19; Revelation 19:7-9;21:9 (KJV)

Chapter 2 - Finding Out Who You Are
A Bible Character 113
Luke 22:47, 57, 60; 23:21-34; Mark 15:1, 10-11; 16:1; Matthew 21:24; 1 Peter 2:9 (KJV)
The Brightest Light 116
Matthew 5:14-16 (KJV)
If Thou Be.. 117
Luke 4:1-13 (KJV)
I'm Not Lucky – I'm Blessed 118
Genesis 12:3, 26:4; Deuteronomy 7:3-14 (KJV)
It is Your Destiny 120
Psalms 139:1-6; 14-18 (KJV)
Scariest Journey 121
Luke 17:21; John 14:6 (KJV)
Simply Because You Are Mine 122
Matthew 7:11; 1 Corinthians 2:9-11; Isaiah 64:4; Psalms 31:19 (KJV)

Chapter 3 – Encouragement
Be Not Afraid, Only Believe 124
Mark 5:35-43 (KJV)
Be Still! 125
Psalms 46:10 (KJV)
Good News 126
1 Corinthians 15:3, 15:52; Mark 13:24-27; Revelation 1:7, 19:7-9, 20:1-3, 21:1-5 (KJV)
Happy is the Woman or Man 128
Proverbs 3:1-18 (KJV)
Hero in You 130
John 15:13 (KJV)

It's Alright 131
  James 1:5 (KJV)
Your Gifts and Talents 132
  Job 33:6; Isaiah 29:16; 45:9; 64:8; Matthew 6:10; 25:45 (KJV)

Chapter 4 – Words of Advice
Back Talk 134
  Ephesians 2:2; 2 Chronicles 30:8; 1 Peter 1:2 (KJV)
Doin' the Israelite 135
  Exodus 11:2; 13:21; 14:27-28; 16:2-3,12; 17:2-4 (KJV)
Forgive or Forgive Not 137
  Luke 6:37; Mark 11:25-26 (KJV)
Garbage in Garbage Out! 138
  Philippians 4:8-9 (KJV)
If You Want To Make God Laugh! 139
  Proverbs 19:21; Matthew 5:36; Isaiah 46:9-11 (KJV)
Lean Not 140
  Proverbs 3:5-6; James 1:5 (KJV)
Love is An Action 141
  Philippians 4:19 (KJV)

Chapter 5 – Fighting the Enemy
But for Your Praying Saints 143
  Ephesians 6:18; 1 Thessalonians 5:17; James 5:16 (KJV)
Idols, Idols, Idols 144
  1 John 5:21 (KJV)
It's War! 145
  Ephesians 6:10-17 (KJV)
Just Do It! 146
  Mark 16:15-20 (KJV)
The Perfect Murder 147
  Romans 7:14-21 (KJV)
Put it All On! 148
  Ephesians 6:11-17 (KJV)
What's His Face? 149
  Genesis 3:15; John 19:11 (KJV)

Chapter 6 – Those Bible People

Follow the Anointing 151
   1 Samuel 18:1-4, 20:14-17; 2 Samuel 1:11-12, 17, 25-27 (KJV)
Here I Am 153
   1 Samuel 3 (KJV)
Highly Favored 155
   Luke 1:27-38 (KJV)
Joseph 156
   Genesis 37:2-5, 9, 15; 31-35; 41:41-43; 45:1-5 (KJV)
Just Said No 158
   Daniel 3:1-6 (KJV)
She Was First 159
   John 20:1-18; Luke 24:1-10; Mark 16:1-11; Matthew 28:1-8 (KJV)
So Be Like Job 163
   Job 1:1, 8-12; 2:1-6; 42:12-13 (KJV)

Chapter 7 – The Movies: Their Spiritual Messages

The Circle of Life 166
   Genesis 4:1-11; 33:4,10-11 (KJV)
E.T. 168
   John 14:1-4 (KJV)
If You Build It 169
   1 Samuel 15:22; Hebrews 11:6; John 10:27; Philippians 2:13; Ephesians 1:9 (KJV)
May the Force 170
   1 Corinthians 13:4-7 (KJV)
The Mummy's Curse 171
   Romans 6:6-7 (KJV)
The Red Pill or the Blue 172
   John 10:10; Romans 12:2-3; Proverbs 9:10 (KJV)
The Richest Man in Town 173
   John 15:13; Matthew 6:19; Proverbs 18:22; Psalms 91:11 (KJV)

Scriptural Index 174

Poems

Chapter 1 -
The Father, Son, and Holy Spirit

Ain't He All That! 1
He's Good At 2
Master of Masters 3
Pieces of Myself 5
Somethin' Told Me 7
That Small Still Voice 9
With His Own Blood 11

Dr. Lydia A. Woods

Ain't He All That!

Hebrews 1:2-3; John 1:1-5; Revelation 22:13 (KJV)
Scripture Reference on page 102

You've heard the young people say...
That he or she ain't all that,
I know One who's All That and that's a fact.

Ain't He All That – and then some.
He's Alpha Omega the Holy One.

Ain't He All That – and that's for sure,
Sent for the salvation of man – Earth's cure.

Ain't He All That – and you know why,
Cause He's the only One that can satisfy.

Ain't He All That – just look around and attest,
He's head and heels over all the rest.

Ain't He All That – He can take away pain,
Heal broken hearts, save sinners with no strain.

Ain't He All That – a place to safely run,
In times of trouble, He's the only one.

Ain't He All That – for the care and love,
He's All that – Our Father above!

Well now that you have the final fact,
You can tell for yourself – Ain't He All That!

He's Good At

Genesis 1:3, 9, 12, 16, 24, 27, 31; Isaiah 14:27, 46:9-11 (KJV)
Scripture Reference on page 103

He's good you've got to give it to Him,
He didn't need help creating angels, man, or cherubim,

He's good cause He made all that you see,
Canyons, flowers, bugs, rivers, and seas.

He's good at making the sun,
The moon, skies and stars every one,

He's good at making mountains and lakes,
He's just good for goodness sake,

He's good at making women and men,
And loving them in spite of their sin,

He's good at accomplishing all His plans,
Through the lives of all humankind.

He's good at what He does,
That's why we are here and He's above.

He's good at solving our little messes,
That He turns into our greatest successes.

He's good at blessing us too,
I'm trying to figure how -- He do what He do!

He's good all the time and that's a fact!
So just give it up cause -- He's Good At!

Dr. Lydia A. Woods

Master of Masters

Matthew 4:1; 4:19; 5:1-2; 7:29; 8:26; 11:5; Luke 8:43-48; John 2:6-9; 11:43-44 (KJV)
Scripture Reference on page 105

The Master of Masters was a fisher of men,
He taught the people and forgave all their sin.

He was tempted of Satan in the wilderness,
But full of the Spirit He did resist.

He was pressed by the multitude from all around,
On the mountain He taught, and made the Word profound.

He delivered the sick from all their pain,
He broke down the law and made it plain.

He made the blind to see and He calmed the rain,
And healed the minds of those insane.

He turned the water to wine, at the wedding feast,
He sent foul, filthy spirits into the beast.

A woman with faith who believed in Him,
And did not believe her chances were dim.

Under the Rainbow

Touched the hem of His garment and she got blessed,
And captured the virtue He did possess.

Now it's written all there in His Holy Book,
Just open it up and have a look.

He raised the dead to life, and made the lame to walk,
He spent time with His disciples, and they did talk.

About eternal life and the Father above,
And of that greatest commandment - How to Love.

He spoke in parables, so only they would know,
The ones with ears, could learn and grow.

Who open their hearts, and the Son accept,
And repent of their sins, which gives Him respect.

Cause He's the Master of Masters, the Holy One,
The Alpha and Omega, God's Beloved Son!

Master of Masters

Dr. Lydia A. Woods

Pieces of Myself

Hebrews 13:5; Romans 12:3; Ephesians 4:7 (KJV)
Scripture Reference on page 108

I've placed pieces of Myself within your heart,
I'm calling you home after we've been apart.

You on earth and Me in heaven above,
We'll be joined again through our Love.

You will hear My gentle calling- search for Me,
Out of darkness into My light – now you will see.

That I've never left you alone, I'm always there,
You are under My protection and constant care.

Pieces of Myself in my children's hearts,
Soon we'll be together and never again to part!

Dr. Lydia A. Woods

Somethin' Told Me

John 12:26; Ephesians 4:30; Luke 2:26 (KJV)
Scripture Reference on page 109

Somethin' told me,
I should have turned left when I turned right,
Somethin' told me,
I should have called her late last night,

Somethin' told me,
Not to say those unkind words,
Somethin' told me,
That my bill was due on the third,

Somethin' told me,
That you were not doing so well,
Somethin' told me,
That I could get that dress at the mall on sale,

Somethin' told me,
Not to pick up that phone or go into that room,
Somethin' told me,
That he wasn't the right bridegroom.

If I had a dollar,
For all the times I've heard,
But did not heed the gentle voice,
Or the light urging words,

Of the faint and fleeting sound,
Within my being,
Somethin' told me,
Without my knowing or my seeing.

The Somethin' told me,
One day not long ago,
Will you stop saying,
"Somethin'" told you so and so,

My name is not "Somethin,'"
Please call my name out right,
My name is Holy Spirit,
And I live within you out of sight.

I was sent by my Master,
To lead and guide you into truth,
My job is to protect you,
And bring you to remembrance, Do you need proof?

Just open up His Word,
And read about Me for yourself,
My name is not "Somethin,'"
But I'm your Lord - it's Me Myself!

Somethin' Told Me

Dr. Lydia A. Woods

That Small Still Voice

1 Kings 19:11-12; Hebrews 3:7 (KJV)
Scripture Reference on page 110

That small still voice,
You've heard it now and then.
But you can hear it often,
If you stop and listen my friend.

The noise and speed at which you move,
Stop running here and there.
Makes it impossible to hear,
Music, sounds, and noise everywhere.

The enemy wants you very busy,
So strung out with stress and cares.
In a world that moves at fast pace,
And keeps your mind going everywhere.

That small still voice,
It is small not big at all,
And still means not moving,
Think back and just recall.

When last you heard the Voice,
So clear that it seemed quite real,
You were in a quiet place,
Your mind and body were still.

So, take moments in your day,
Come away my beloved child,
Sit quietly beside me,
And hear My small still voice awhile.

Come away my beloved child,
Take time from the confusion - come away,
I am always speaking to you,
In a small still voice – That's My way!

That Small Still Voice

Dr. Lydia A. Woods

With His Own Blood

Acts 20:28; Hosea 2:19; Revelation 19:7-9; 21:9 (KJV)
Scripture Reference on page 111

I love a love story, as most women do.
Give me a happy ending, plus boxes of tissue too.

I'll cry you a bucket, in the dark of any show.
Cause a love story pulls, at my heart strings, anyway you go.

Well, the greatest love story ever written, I know of in this life,
Is the love of Jesus Christ for the church – His sought-after wife.

The most romantic thing I know, is a man laying down His life,
For the woman that He love, for His precious, beloved wife.

The horrible death that He suffered, so that His beloved could only live,
Is the most beautiful gift of Love that anyone can give.

My favorite hymn ever, I've loved it since a child.
The melody sweetly haunts me, as I hum the tune awhile.

"From heaven He came and sought her, to be His holy bride,
With His own blood He brought her, and for her life He died."

But not like Romeo and Juliet, star-crossed lovers in that tale,
That only in death, can they together dwell.

Our love story is unsurpassed, for not even death can hold,
This lover in the grave, that's how this story goes.

The ending tells, of the greatest victory won,
For God so loved the world, He gave His only Son.

After giving up His life, for His beloved precious Bride,
He is raised again to life, and awaits her by His side!

Chapter 2 - Finding Out Who You Are

A Bible Character 15
The Brightest Light 17
If Thou Be... 19
I'm Not Lucky – I'm Blessed 21
It is Your Destiny 22
Scariest Journey 23
Simply Because You Are Mine..25

Dr. Lydia A. Woods

A Bible Character

Luke 22:47, 57, 60; 23:21-34; Mark 15:1,10-11,16:1
Matthew 21:24; 1 Peter 2:9 (KJV)
Scripture Reference on page 113

I've heard the Holy Book called the, "Living Word,"
It lives and breathes, and strains to be heard.
And I heard a Saint say, I'd like to be,
A Bible character for all to see.

No sooner said, than the chance came their way,
The Word leapt from the page to the everyday.
And all of a sudden that Word came alive,
The Holy Spirit had heard, and opportunity arrived.

It's an honor to be on the battlefield,
In the perilous days when warfare is real.
We'll all get our chance to stand for Christ,
And prove to everyone that we're brought with a price.

Which character will you be on that Bible stage,
If the casting is done and war is waged?
Are you Judas, who comes with kisses by night,
Or Pilot who washes the blood out of sight?

Are you in the crowd crying crucify Him,
Or Peter who denies that he is His friend?
Or the soldiers who cast lots for His garment in greed,
Or the wicked leaders who arranged the deed?

Under the Rainbow

Are you one of the twelve who walked with Him
But couldn't be found when the evening grew dim?
Were you one of the women, He delivered from sin,
But remembered that He said, "He would rise again?"

Even though they were afraid, they went to the tomb,
To give honor to their Lord and His body groom.
Will you be counted with the very few,
Who waited on the Lord as their hope grew?

And believed all He'd said would come true,
That He would return for me and you.
And in the meantime, while we're on earth,
Washed in His blood, a child of new birth.

Just check yourself out in every way,
And see which role you'll play today.
Could they cast you for peculiar people indeed,
The Royal Priesthood and Child of His seed?

Called by His name and set aside,
The Temple of God, let His Spirit abide.
In the beauty of Holiness tried and true,
Let His Spirit be found in me and you.

A Bible Character

Dr. Lydia A. Woods

The Brightest Light

Matthew 5:14-16 (KJV)
Scripture Reference on page 116

God places His brightest light in the darkest place,
The light begins to shine in the - darkness face.
The brightest light has not a clue,
Of what it is really meant to do.

It just shines that's all it knows,
Its light just follows wherever it goes.
The light travels here and there,
In and out and everywhere.

The light does not care much for the dark,
For light is pure within its heart.
God's children are the light in the earth.
Their light begins with their new birth.

It is a glorious light they cannot see,
Others except that the light must be.
So believe in your light never fear,
The darkness recognizes who you are my dear.

Darkness flees when the light is around,
Darkness is full of fear that abounds.
The light reflects the truth of God's Son,
And the glorious victory He has won.

To bring kingdom on earth is the plan.
Light will illuminate the path of man.
Jesus speaks of Himself as the light,
And those that believe have inherited the right.

To be filled with His Spirit and baptized with fire,
It's what this earthly mission requires.
So, know that the world needs your light,
And guard it as your precious birthright.

Hide it not under a bushel or bed.
You are the light of the world, so the Bible said.
Jesus is the Truth, the Life, and the Way,
Add your light to His glorious purpose today!

Dr. Lydia A. Woods

If Thou Be...

Luke 4:1-13 (KJV)
Scripture Reference on page 117

If thou be the Son of God,
Satan's question to Jesus -- Now that was odd!

Satan Knew He was the only Begotten Son,
Was he just fooling around, having a bit of fun!

Is Satan so stupid or something worse,
To expect Jesus to serve him and His Father curse!

Jesus came to do the Father's will,
And Satan knew it -- so what's the deal!

Now I've always thought Satan, not to bright,
To question Jesus on the issue of His birthright,

And if he would question Jesus with so stupid a plan,
Then he'll put the question to any ordinary man.

Under the Rainbow

Yes, Satan questions our birthright day in and out,
Trying to cause confusion and set up doubt.

And his stupid plan has worked like a charm,
Saints are giving him power and being disarmed.

His questioning their birthright has caused many to doubt,
They have the power to foil his plan and wipe him out.

Power given to them through the Holy Name,
Step up with faith and your birthright claim.

So that whosoever believes in Him,
Can through faith in Jesus their salvation win.

And when Satan questions - If Thou Be ...?
Say, it is written - there is no doubt in me!

If Thou Be...

Dr. Lydia A. Woods

I'm Not Lucky – I'm Blessed

Genesis 12:3, 26:4; Deuteronomy 7:3-14 (KJV)
Scripture Reference on page 118

I tell people all the time,
I'm not lucky – I'm blessed.
Luck is a word the world uses,
But blessed is the term I prefer to confess.

Lucky is not in the vocabulary of God's Word,
Saints rid luck from your conversation today.
It's only God's grace and mercy,
That follows us as we journey in life's way.

Lucky is a term of Satan,
It involves witchcraft and chances of fate.
But promises of God's blessings to His children,
It's not magic, but a sure and solid mandate.

We live in the showering of His blessings,
We walk in grace and mercy from hour to hour.
Miracles are just everyday occurrences,
It's our birthright to live our lives in His power.

The power of His Word,
That transcends every wicked device,
There is power in our tongues,
Saints lets correct our speech, that's my advice.

Remember that it is not luck,
That comes and goes at Satan's whim,
But the state of our existence,
When we walk by Faith in Him.

It is Your Destiny

Psalms 139:1-6; 14-18 (KJV)
Scripture Reference on page 120

Don't take your gifts for granted,
They come so easily to you.
You were born with special talents,
Others would kill for what you do.

You can't believe that you are special.
Although many have said it to you,
Unique in all the world,
When will you believe that it is true?

It is scary to wonder,
About the gifts that lay inside,
Could I really be that Person?
Does greatness in me abide?

Believe that God has made you,
Special and unique indeed,
Place your future in His hands,
For this greatness to succeed.

It is your final destiny,
For greatness to achieve,
I hope these words encourage you,
To in yourself believe!

Dr. Lydia A. Woods

Scariest Journey

Luke 17:21; John 14:6 (KJV)
Scripture Reference on page 121

The scariest journey you will ever take,
Is inside yourself, begin do not wait.

You've been running fast the other way,
Your life is busy – just stop today.

Turn the TV off, cut the music too,
Computer, answering machine - You know what to do.

You're afraid of the silence of your mind,
You are afraid of what you will find.

Take this trip I guarantee you will find,
What you are looking for – peace of mind.

Stop looking for God on the outside,
For it is in your heart that He abides.

He will talk to you from on the inside,
But it is only you who can decide.

You are moving like a wriggling child,
Be still – sit still - and meditate a while.

Take that scary journey it's not so bad,
What you'll find it's truer than what you had!

Dr. Lydia A. Woods

Simply Because You Are Mine

Matthew 7:11; 1 Corinthians 2:9-11; Isaiah 64:4; Psalms 31:19 (KJV)
Scripture Reference on page 122

Have you ever been blessed by the Lord?

I have, so many times I can't even count.
And it was one day recently that I found out,
A mystery that was hidden from me,
I was blinded, and I didn't really see.

A truth that I had heard many times and should know,
That Jesus loves me, for the Bible tells me so,
But we only really know in part,
And can't truly understand until He expands our heart.

And it was on that day the Lord blessed me well,
My heart was full, and the tears began to swell.
He blessed me with the secrets of my Heart,
Only He and I knew about this part.

You see, I didn't have a revelation of the depth of His love,
And revelation knowledge comes from His Spirit above.

So, one day the Lord spoke softly to me,
"I don't bless you because you are so good,
Or because you always behave as you should,
I bless you because I am true and just and kind,
I bless you simply because you are mine."

He said,
"Think of how you bless your children at Christmas time,
You plan for weeks for the day when you can make their faces shine.
How much more do I too plan for mine,
Hoping to see their faces shine?"

"Do you think that I am one who does not feel?
Sometimes, I think you don't believe, I am real.
I've been working to prove to you every day,
By providing your needs and wants in every way.

That I love you, not because you are so good,
Or because you always behave as you should,
But because I am true and just and kind,
And Simply Because You Are Mine."

Simply Because You Are Mine

Chapter 3 – Encouragement

Be Not Afraid, Only Believe 29
Be Still! 30
Good News 31
Happy is the Woman or Man..33
Hero in You 34
It's Alright 35
Your Gifts and Talents 36

Dr. Lydia A. Woods

Be Not Afraid, Only Believe

Mark 5:35-43 (KJV)
Scripture Reference on page 124

You know fear drives faith right out of our hearts,
And it's great faith that will set you apart.

The ruler of the synagogue found this out that day,
When he went to ask help of Jesus along the way.

Then a message came that his daughter had just died,
He need not trouble the master – his servant cried.

"Be not afraid, only believe," Jesus said,
Jesus knew that He could raise her from that sick bed.

When Jesus came to the house, they laughed Him to scorn,
He said, "she is just sleeping do not weep and mourn."

Clearing the house, He took His disciples into her room,
Commanding her to rise He dispelled all sadness and gloom.

Straightway the damsel arose and began to walk,
You know everyone was excited and began to talk.

How could the master this great feat achieve?
If you will, Be Not Afraid, Only Believe!

Be Still!

Psalms 46:10 (KJV)
Scripture Reference on page 125

As a child of God, He often says to me,
Child "Be Still," just wait and see.
I hate it when He say, "Be Still,"
Cause my flesh is jumpin' – That's against my will.

He means, "Be Still," in your flesh, and mouth, and mind,
Just sit yourself down on your behind.

The nature of a child is to move about,
Running here and there trying to figure things out.
Just what to do about this and that,
That's true about kids and that's a fact.

So, when the Father says to "Be Still,"
He means that we are to submit our will,
The very thing that you want to do,
Put I on the shelf, like He told you to.

He has a plan for the problem already in hand,
Before you were born, because He "Is the Man,"
In heaven and earth it's always His will,
So, will you just sit down and "Be Still!"

Dr. Lydia A. Woods

Good News

1 Corinthians 15:3, 15:52; Mark 13:24-27;
Revelation 1:7, 19:7-9;20:1-3, 21:1-5 (KJV)
Scripture Reference on page 126

Jesus died on the cross, for our souls,
He took our sickness in His body, so it was told.

That's how it all began a long time ago,
I'm not telling no tales that you don't know.

Brothers and sisters, you better listen up,
And take a long cool drink from the Jesus cup.

It's time we all got saved, in these terrible times,
You know the raptures comin', don't be left behind.

He's comin' in the clouds, in a twinkle of an eye,
You know the Saints that are living, will not die.

So, believe in Him and in the power of His might,
Cause He's coming like a thief, in the night.

Then there's seven long years, of hell on earth,
It's the tribulation times, Thank God for His Birth!

Cause the Saints will be rockin' at the marriage feast,
And those here on earth will be fighting the beast.

Under the Rainbow

He's coming back to set up His reign,
The earth will be changed, it won't be the same.

We're all coming back as Kings and Priest,
We won't have to contend with the beast.

He'll be sitting in the pit, with all of his gang,
Until Jesus is finished with His thousand-year reign.

Then Satan watch out cause yo' end is near,
The lake of fire is what you fear.

Now I'm telling the truth of what the scriptures say,
There's a Holy New Jerusalem on its way.

God will dwell with men on this new earth,
No sorrow will exist in this new birth.

So, get your heart right and set your mind,
And get Salvation now and put your sins behind.

I'm spreading the Good News throughout the Land,
That Jesus Christ, He is our Man!
That Jesus Christ, He is our Man!
That Jesus Christ, He is our Man!

Good News

Dr. Lydia A. Woods

Happy is the Woman or Man

Proverbs 3:1-18 (KJV)
Scripture Reference on page 128

Happy is the woman or man,
That findeth wisdom in his hand.

For wisdom is better that silver or fine gold,
More precious that rubies, so I am told.

More precious than all things you could desire,
So, it's to wisdom that I'll aspire.

Ways of pleasantness – paths of peace,
Let not your pursuit of wisdom ever cease.

Honor and riches – length of days,
Like a tree of life bind and save.

Forget not His law, bind it tight,
Happy is the woman or man who gets this right!

Hero in You

John 15:13 (KJV)
Scripture Reference on page 130

Deep in the recesses of the human heart,
A hero lives – ready to do their part.

You cannot tell by looking at the outward man,
If the hero lives there – and can withstand.

For the hero comes in all sizes and shapes,
And in an instant knows the action they will take.

For the hero lives within out of sight,
Waiting to come forth to test their might.

To know if they are brave or not,
A challenge must come to test them on the spot.

When opportunity comes – into action they spring,
There is no time to think – the hero must do that thing.

The hero never hesitates to consider self,
Never thinks of the danger – only has to help.

The helpless victim or to right a wrong,
Never wants a reward or a hero's song.

The Word says that no greater love has man in the end,
Than to lay down their life for a stranger or friend.

Many opportunities lay in your path today,
Don't let them pass you by along life's way.

Let the Hero perform in times of need,
Showing love to one another is our Christian creed.

Dr. Lydia A. Woods

It's Alright

James 1:5 (KJV)
Scripture Reference on page 131

I am like the kid who pesters their mother,
And father and sisters and even their brothers.
Wanting answers to every mysterious wonder,
So many questions – I like to ponder.

I want to know how a tree grows so high?
How many stars are in the sky?
How does a hummingbird really fly?
Mother, mother please tell me why?

And with the Lord I am just the same,
I pray and pray and call His name.
Wanting answers to problems, clear vision, and sight,
But all He says, sometimes is, "It's Alright."

And when I get the "It's Alright." response, it's quite profound,
There is something inside me that settles down.
A peace that floods my very being,
I know the problem is solved without my seeing.

I am coming to know the Father well,
And about Him to everyone I tell,
About His answers as we talk – that's quite,
Soothing to my spirit each time I hear, "It's Alright."

Your Gifts and Talents

Job 33:6; Isaiah 29:16; 45:9; 64:8; Matthew 6:10; 25:45 (KJV)
Scripture Reference on page 132

That gift or talent of yours is not for you,
So, find out what you are supposed to do.

Why did God make you special - just so.
Wouldn't you really like to know?

You are the vessel fashioned by His hand,
To be used of the Master - the purpose of this plan.

Take that gift use it as the Lord Wills,
Blessing others with your talents and skills.

Just imagine a world where this is so,
People blessing one another – that's awesome you know.

The Master's purpose is for His Kingdom to come on earth,
By using our gifts and talents – which justifies our birth!

Chapter 4 – Words of Advice

Back Talk 39
Doin' the Israelite 41
Forgive or Forgive Not 44
Garbage in Garbage Out!..45
If You Want To Make God Laugh! 47
Lean Not 49
Love is An Action 50

Dr. Lydia A. Woods

Back Talk

Ephesians 2:2; 2 Chronicles 30:8; 1 Peter 1:2 (KJV)
Scripture Reference on page 134

In the old days children knew well,
You didn't give no "Back Talk," I'm here to tell.

That hand would come up – You'd be on the floor,
Or running to try to reach the door.

You did what you were told – no "Back Talk" then,
But times have changed, and we are deeper in sin.

Children "Back Talk" their parents' every day,
Questioning everything the parents have to say.

And I realize that we even "Back Talk" God,
We are not obedient children – what could be more odd?

We don't just do what we are told,
We are not obedient or submissive – just bold!

Things have gotten completely out of hand,
Disobedience is rampant among God's children.

Under the Rainbow

Stiff-necked is what the Bible tells,
Started with Satan – now he dwells in hell.

Those of us who hear God's small still voice,
Need not question "Why" – we have no choice.

Behind perfect obedience a blessing waits,
Lets be quick to respond, don't hesitate.

There is a blessing for others when we act,
Especially for the obedient child and that's a fact.

So, don't miss out on any of your blessings child,
Perfect obedience brings joy and makes others smile!

Dr. Lydia A. Woods

Doin' the Israelite

Exodus 11:2, 13:21, 14:27-28, 16:2-3, 12, 17:2-4 (KJV)
Scripture Reference on page 135

Have you ever thought after reading about?
How the Lord brought the Israelites out,
Just how they could murmur and complain,
It boggles my mind and spins my brain.

I call it, "Doin' the Israelite!"

I couldn't imagine after all God had done,
Wanting to turn back, high tail it and run,
Back to bondage and the Pharaoh's whip,
And not wanting to make that glorious trip.

I call it, "Doin' the Israelite!"

After bringing them out with silver and gold,
Every man, woman, child from the young to the old,
After parting the sea and walking on dry land,
And destroying the enemy with a sweep of His hand.

I call it, "Doin' the Israelite!"

How could they slip back to their ungodly way?
While Moses was getting what God had to say,
On the tablets of stone, God's glorious Word,
Of which His people had never heard.

I call it, "Doin' the Israelite!"

Now, remember how He led them, by night and by day,
Leading them so evident all of the way,
And all of the miracles and the wondrous feats,
Water from stone and manna to eat.

I call it, "Doin' the Israelite!"

He kept them better than the birds or the lilies of the field,
It's hard to comprehend; it can't really be real,
But now as I take my wilderness walk,
Sometimes, I have to check my thoughts and my talk.

Am I, "Doin' the Israelite!"

I find that I too, murmur and complain,
And sometimes I think I'll go insane,
I know the Spirit of God dwells in me,
And I should walk by faith unable to see.

Am I, "Doin' the Israelite!"

It isn't as easy, as it looks,
I thought it would be, after reading His book,
His account of the Israelites warns all of us,
Of the possible fate it we doubt and mistrust.

Are you, "Doin' the Israelite!"

Saints believe what I am about to say,
You will do the Israelite every day,
Yes, I'm telling it right and telling it straight,
We are all filled, with fear, mistrust, and hate.

Are you, "Doin' the Israelite!"

Doin' the Israelite

Dr. Lydia A. Woods

Lord, help and forgive me, I repent and ask,
For strength and understanding, so I can last,
The entire way to the Promise land,
Don't leave me in the wilderness; bring me out by your hand.

I don't want to be caught, "Doin' the Israelite!"

Lord I want to be found steadfast and true,
Faithful to the end, believing in You,
You never said, it would be easy or a piece of cake,
But that tribulation would come, and it's for our sakes.

I am growing in faith every day,
I believe you will perfect me in every way,
But it's not because I am so good,
Or because I have faith like I should.

But because, you are faithful and true to Your Word,
And what You have started, you'll finish, I've heard.
And in the end, everything will be right,
And I won't be caught, "Doin' the Israelite!"

Forgive or Forgive Not

Luke 6:37; Mark 11:25-26 (KJV)
Scripture Reference on page 137

Forgive or forgive not, the choice is up to you.
But choose wisely and carefully whatever you do!

For to forgive not - can seal your very fate,
By eating you alive, with a cancer of consuming hate.

But for to forgive - now you're talking my language here,
The sweetest of gestures, frees your Spirit, my dear!

Dr. Lydia A. Woods

Garbage in Garbage Out!

Philippians 4:8 (KJV)
Scripture Reference on page 138

Garbage in, garbage out,
What the heck are they talking about?

Who would put garbage where it doesn't belong?
Doesn't everyone know this is wrong?

But garbage goes into the temple every day,
In through the ears and eyes, that's the way.

Garbage like violence, music, gossip, and such,
This world of Garbage is just too much!

When garbage goes in then what comes out?
People acting out violence, and hate, no doubt.

Children killing each other - folks hating their neighbor,
Man's inhumanity toward man that's the going flavor.

Keep violence, music, gossip off your plate,
Garbage in Garbage out – It is not too late!

Dr. Lydia A. Woods

If You Want To Make God Laugh!

Proverbs 19:21; Matthew 5:36; Isaiah 46:9-11 (KJV)
Scripture Reference on page 139

The old folk used to say, "It's all in God's Hands,"
And if you want to make God laugh,
Just tell Him your plans!

That you're gonna do this and that,
You're over twenty-one and that's a fact,
You're big and bad, so much in control,
Do what you want cause you're grown and bold.

The world taught you well about the planning part,
Everybody does it, and that's being smart.
To become a responsible adult and grown,
You must get on the go, get a plan of your own.

The sooner you realize that you have no power,
To make things happen from hour to hour,
That you can't change one hair on your head,
That you didn't wake yourself up today to get out of bed.

Under the Rainbow

That you're a little child who can't come in or go out,
It doesn't do any good to get mad or pout.
Things are out of your control so get with the plan,
That everything is purposed by God's own hand.

You were brought with a price,
Do you know what that means?
You have got to give it up,
No use making a scene.

Scripture says many are the plans of a man,
But God's purposes will prevail throughout the land,
Stop drowning in the sea of denial,
Cause you're bound to Him all the while.

So, if you want to make God laugh today,
Just open your mouth, let Him hear you say,
That you've got plans and you're gonna do this and that,
And Watch the Hand of God just slap you Back!

Dr. Lydia A. Woods

Lean Not

Proverbs 3:5-6; James 1:5 (KJV)
Scripture Reference on page 140

Lean not to thy own understanding,
For you haven't got all the facts.
Take if from the one who knows all,
For your understanding is feeble and lacks.

It lacks, the wisdom of the ages,
It lacks, because you're not full grown.
It lacks, because your wisdom is fuzzy.
It lack, because of sin that is sown.

I know you made good grades in school.
You've always been told that you are smart.
But your intellect is no good in this realm,
In the Spirit it's faith that sets you apart.

So, take your understanding from the Father,
He is wise and has your best interest at heart,
He knows that you are a child just stumbling,
He is willing to pick you up and take your part.

So, lean not to thy own understanding,
Ask for wisdom, He will give it freely to you.
For His thoughts and His ways are much higher,
But it's His understanding that will see you through!

Love is An Action

Philippians 4:19 (KJV)
Scripture Reference on page 141

*The Child asked the Mother, "Mommy, do you love me?
You didn't tell me today, where is your love, I just don't see?"*

My darling child, I told you a hundred times today,
Did you not hear me? - I said, "I love you in every way."

I told you, I loved you by waking you up,
In preparing your meals and filling your cup.

In providing the roof, over your head,
By turning on the heat as you slept in your bed.

By driving you to school, giving lunch money and a kiss,
By giving you a hug, whenever you insist.

In combing your hair, and washing your clothes,
And listening to your tales of junior high woes.

Helping with your homework, watching the game that you won,
By telling you no... till your chores were all done.

For my darling, love isn't just words that you say,
Love is an Action – that you show every day!

So, if you are wondering if God really loves you,
Look at your life and see if it's true.

For you are His darling child, He said, "I love you, today,"
Cause "Love is an Action", that He shows every day!

Chapter 5 – Fighting the Enemy

But for Your Praying Saints 53
Idols, Idols, Idols 55
It's War! 57
Just Do It! 59
The Perfect Murder 61
Put it All On! 63
What's His Face? 65

Dr. Lydia A. Woods

But for Your Praying Saints

Ephesians 6:18; 1 Thessalonians 5:17; James 5:16 (KJV)
Scripture Reference on page 143

Look out Satan 'cause you've been uncovered,
The truths been told by my spiritual brother.
Frank Peretti is the saint that's blessed me well,
He reveals what's going on in the pit of hell.

When he reads his book,
"This Present Darkness," on Cassette,
I am telling you saints you will never regret.
Listening to this book will spiritually educate you.
It will give you insight on just what to do.

His book is all about Satan's demons as they plot and plan,
To destroy God's saints and steal the souls of man.
But don't despair the Lord's warriors are in place,
He dispatches angelic forces, and they are on the case.

Their weapons are mighty for strongholds come down,
And they are powered by saints that aren't playing around.
He speaks of saints who know just what to do,
Using the power of prayer as they were commanded to.

As those mighty prayers ascend to the throne,
They empower the angels and they make right the wrong.
They can take out satanic demons left and right,
They make quick work of them in this spiritual fight.

My daughter and I play the tape over and over again,
We love to hear the ending, when the angels win.
And then there's our favorite line in all of the book,
As the demon breaths his last and takes one long look.

At the captain of the host his angelic enemy,
Now here's the part that thrills my daughter and me,
Before he is vanquished, he speaks deep and faint,
But for your praying saints…

Dr. Lydia A. Woods

Idols, Idols, Idols

1 John 5:21 (KJV)
Scripture Reference on page 144

Idols for sale so step right up don't wait,
No life should be without one they are really great!

One in every bedroom, office, or den,
And definitely in the workplace my friend.

One in blue, or white, or red,
In the bathroom, closet, and by your bed.

Idols help you to work or play,
Idols help you relax and look good too - I must say.

They come in big, small, short, or tall,
Get them on sale or in the mall,

Keep them in the garage or on a chair,
Eat it, touch it, or wear it in your hair.

Under the Rainbow

Made of gold, silver, wood, or tin,
Buy one or two for yourself or even a friend.

They also come in metal, cloth, or liquid and such,
You can never have enough or too much.

Animal, plant, mineral it doesn't matter,
Idols, Idols, Idols just gather and gather.

Idols here and idols there,
There are seasons for idols everywhere.

Get to the point of what you're trying to say,
What are these stupid idols anyway?

Idols, Idols, Idols

Dr. Lydia A. Woods

It's War!

Ephesians 6:10-17 (KJV)
Scripture Reference on page 145

It's War!
When you take Jesus and you're reborn,
There's something you should know, that's going on.

It's War!
In high places that you can't see,
Put on your Spiritual ears, and listen to me.

It's War!
Yeah, its war, that I'm talking about,
When I am finished there will be no doubt.

It's War!
Against darkness and wickedness on high,
If you listen well there's no fear you'll die!

It's War!
But the victory's yours, without a doubt,
Your Savior fought the fight and worked it all out.

It's War!
But there is a special way you fight,
You just stand still with all of your might.

It's War!
And there's a special armor you wear,
The helmet of Salvation won't muster your hair.

It's War!

Under the Rainbow

And on your loins the Truth you'll wear,
The Breastplate of Righteousness won't even tear.

You have the Gospel of Peace upon your feet,
And with the Shield in hand you won't feel the heat,

From the wicked fiery darts being thrown at you,
You don't have to despair, you know what to do.

With the Sword in hand just lift it high,
And quench those darts and watch them fly.

But you're not hurt, you only have to stand,
And be very patient and wait on your Man.

Cause He's coming in a cloud to rescue you,
The Holy One of God, Tried and True.

It's War!
And you're commanded to watch and pray,
I can hear the Lord say on that final day,

Well done good soldier - come on in,
Did you have a doubt that we would win!

And in the end, you'll be proud to say,
I had my armor on and withstood the evil day.

It's War!

Dr. Lydia A. Woods

Just Do It!

Mark 16:15-20 (KJV)
Scripture Reference on page 146

These signs shall follow them that believe,
Come on Saints, I know that you can read.
I found these signs in Mark sixteen and seventeen,
I didn't read about this in any comic magazine!

It says, to use His name to cast the devil out,
Don't you think that's what Saints should be about?
Jesus cast the devil out while He walked among us,
We should use His name, not fear spirits and trust.

That His Word is true, and there is power in His name,
Keep working that Word you won't be the same.
Now at first it might not look like you're doing a thing,
But in the spirit world you've created a scene.

You have rocked the house where Satan lives,
Keep using the name until Satan gives.
Just keep it up and don't think to quit,
'Cause you're commanded to ....

"Just Do It!"

It also says, with new tongues they will speak.
So get your new tongue, get power, don't be weak.
Tongues edify you not anyone else, you see,
It's evidence of the Holy Spirit in thee.

It's a gift you ask for so make that choice,
Open up your mouth and give the Holy Spirit a voice.
Praying in the Spirit is a more perfect way,
To fulfill what He's commanded us to do every day.

Under the Rainbow

It also builds that faith, and this pleases God,
I know it sounds kind of funny and you look odd.
But remember you're a peculiar people indeed.
Born of His Spirit a child of His seed.

Don't be concerned about how you look,
Cause it's written in His Holy Book.
Just keep it up and don't think to quit,
'

Just Do It!

Dr. Lydia A. Woods

The Perfect Murder

Romans 7:14-21 (KJV)
Scripture Reference on page 147

The perfect murder, I plot at night,
My enemy to put permanently out of sight!

It's ruined my life so it must go,
I'm talking about my will – you know.

I've tried to kill it many times before,
I've kicked it to the curb and out the door.

It won't stay dead or get in line.
But maybe it will stay dead this time!

Cause this time I'm giving it up to the One,
Who's dealt with wills since times begun.

Since killing it is not the way,
I'll give it to God each and every day.

It's not killing that He has in mind,
But little adjustments made over time.

He's slowly lining it up with His own will,
Cause a Will is something you just can't kill.

Dr. Lydia A. Woods

Put it All On!

Ephesians 6:11-17 (KJV)
Scripture Reference on page 148

God said, to put the whole armor on,
It's the gift you get when you're reborn.

Now you probably heard it many times before,
To put it on – don't let Satan in the door.

It's not too big, it fits just right,
'Cause you can't fight on your own might.

The Lord wants you to be able to stand,
In the evil day and take command,

Over Satan's wickedness – Put him under your feet,
It'll give you pleasure; the victory is sweet.

Have you ever thought, what would happen to you,
If you didn't obey, what God told you to do?

That's why many Saints today are laying down,
And pieced of the armor are scattered around.

'Cause they just don't know how to keep it on,
Even though they've been saved are reborn.

Unless it's all on, you won't have success,
You get attacked and your life's a mess.

Those wicked fiery darts keep coming fast,
At times you feel that you won't last.

Just check yourself out a piece is slipping down,
And before you know it, Satan's got you bound.

So, keep the helmet on, you mind to protect.
Darts are aimed there, so you'll lose respect,

For the word of God and His integrity,
He wants to take you joy, so your peace will flee,

And when peace is gone it's confusion there,
Some armor is missing, and you're in despair.

So, renew your mind everyday –
Wash it with the Word, so you can say,

"It is written Satan – Get behind me,"
Experience the Power of the Word and Watch him Flee!

Put it All On!

Dr. Lydia A. Woods

What's His Face?

Genesis 3:15; John 19:11 (KJV)
Scripture Reference on page 149

A very long time ago, so the Bible tells,
A foul rotten thing in heaven did dwell.
He was cast from heaven on that fateful day,
He fell to earth, so the scriptures say.

And in his anger, he began to plot and plan,
To get revenge on God's beloved Man.
In the Garden of Eden he did beguile,
While deceiving Eve all the while.

Then Adam's power over the earth, he did take,
And from that day to this, war on man did make.
But almighty God was just a step ahead,
And sent His Word in the flesh, in mans' stead.

In the flesh He came to save you and me,
They crucified Him so all could see.
And that's where the evil one made, his stupid mistake,
For the life of Jesus, he could not take.

Under the Rainbow

'Cause no sin could be found in the Holy One,
The Lamb of God, His beloved Son.
That's when all of his power over you and me,
Was given back to our Savior, you see.

Now he walks around seeking to destroy,
Anyone who believes they are his toy.
But I'm, here to tell that no power exists,
Over those who would only resist.

And claim Jesus as their Savior, the Holy One,
And believe in Him, their life has just begun.
So, put him under foot when he talks to you,
'Cause you're the Righteousness of God, tried and true.

And He's a thief, a liar, and a big disgrace,
I can't remember his name, you know, "What's his face?"

What's His Face?

Chapter 6 –
Those Bible People

Follow the Anointing 69
Here I Am 71
Highly Favored 73
Joseph 75
Just Said No 79
She Was First 81
So Be Like Job 83

Dr. Lydia A. Woods

Follow the Anointing

1 Samuel 18:1-4, 20:14-17; 2 Samuel 1:11-12, 17, 25-27 (KJV)
Scripture Reference on page 151

Jonathan and David were like brothers, those two,
There was a bond between them that grew and grew.

The scriptures say their souls were knitted together,
And they had much love one for the other.

A covenant between them to seal the love,
With God as their witness in heaven above.

Jonathan gave David his robe, sword, and bow,
A pledge of devotion, that's how covenants go.

Covenants are serious not to be lightly taken,
Bound, one to another can never be forsaken.

David was the anointed, the Spirit of God was with him,
Jonathan knew it because he was closer than a friend.

Under the Rainbow

Their enemies become yours – forever you defend,
To fight for their safety together to the end.

Saul was David's enemy now here is the trick,
Jonathan was Saul's son – so he had to pick!

Once you find the anointing never leave it behind,
Forsaking all others you must follow your mind.

It made me sad when Jonathan was killed,
How could this be a part of God's Will?

Jonathan loved David, why didn't he stay,
Close to the anointing where protection lay?

Follow the anointing stick as close as you can,
This choice will be given to every living woman or man!

Follow the Anointing

Dr. Lydia A. Woods

Here I Am

1 Samuel 3 (KJV)
Scripture Reference on page 153

Samuel was a special child, as most are,
A precious child he was by far.
His mother prayed and she was blessed,
Prayer is powerful I must attest.

For his mother did a thing quite odd,
Gave her precious son back to God.
And in doing so she sealed his fate,
Samuel the first prophet was simply great.

Samuel heard a voice call his name,
He thought it was Eli and did exclaim.
Here am I, I've come to you,
Is there anything that I can do?

Eli told the boy he did not call in the night,
Go back to bed everything's alright.
Two more times the boy heard his name.
He went back to Eli just the same.

Eli realized God's voice is what he heard,
He told Samuel what to do when next it occurred.
Say, "Speak, Lord for your servant hears,"
He instructed the boy and calmed his fears.

When next the Lord called him in the night,
He answered, "Speak, Lord," and it was alright.
The Lord told Samuel many things to say,
This first prophet of God was on his way.

The priest thought Hannah was in her wine,
But it was the prophet "Samuel" on God's mind.
"Here am I," is an excellent response my dears,
And "Speak, Lord, for your servant hears."

Dr. Lydia A. Woods

Highly Favored

Luke 1:26-38 (KJV)
Scripture Reference on page 155

What if one night an Angel visited you?
What in the world would you do?

If he asked you to do a favor for God,
Would it blow you away or sound kind of odd?

Well Mary was visited on that fateful night,
Awaken from sleep to a heavenly sight.

Told that among women she was blessed,
Now here comes Mary's famous test.

Told that she would have a precious son,
Not in the usual way, but the Holy Spirit would come.

A strange and beautiful shadow from on High,
You will be overtaken, and this is why.

To bring forth in thy womb a blessed event,
And call His name Jesus, He is heaven sent!

Sent to heal all mankind and to reconcile,
Us back to God through this blessed child.

Mary agreed as soon as she had heard,
"Be it unto me according to thy word."

This handmaid of God will do what her Lord commands,
Let the record show that by my world I stand.

This lowly handmaiden to bring hope into the world,
This blessed among women, this Hebrew Girl!

Highly Favored

Dr. Lydia A. Woods

Joseph

Genesis 37:2-5, 9, 15; 31-35; 41:41-43; 45:1-5 (KJV)
Scripture Reference on page 156
(Previously published as Coat of Many Colors)

In the Bible there are people, whose stories are told,
I know you think they're outdated and very old.
But there's a lesson to learn for us today,
Let me lay it out in a simple way.

Now take Joseph for instance and what happened to him,
All those brothers who threw him over the rim,
Of that deep dark pit, then plotted his demise,
Joseph hadn't acted cool or very wise.

Jacob loved Joseph more than the others,
This caused a lot of hate in Joseph's brothers.
And beside all that, he made Joseph that coat,
It really made the brothers mad and got their goat.

But that's not all, there's a little more,
Joseph had those dreams, so the brothers evened the score.
Into slavery they sold him on that day,
Dipped the coat in blood and to Jacob did say,

That a wild beast had torn him from limb to limb,
Jacob mourned and grieved for his future was dim.
Cause his precious son was gone never to return,
He rent his clothes – His kin were very concerned.

Under the Rainbow

They could not comfort him, all the daughters and sons,
And that's how Joseph's long journey had begun.
Joseph went through trials and tribulations galore,
He was lied on, thrown in prison, I know his heart was sore.

He missed his father and even those brothers you see,
He had years to work out resentment, to set his soul free.
All through the bad times he held onto his God,
His masters thought him strange and very odd.

But God watched over Joseph for He had a plan,
To bring all Jacob's children to Goshen land.
Not only had Joseph changed, but the brothers too,
Joseph tested them; he gave them back their due.

They were repentive for the evil deed so long ago,
But God turned it to their good, don't you know.
For that's the secret I'm about to reveal to you,
There is one in every family that God works through.

For the salvation of the others, it's a glorious plan,
Are you the one that God has cut out with His hand?
Are you the odd one that never seems to fit in?
Hoping for salvation of all your family in the end?

Joseph

Dr. Lydia A. Woods

Calling on the name of the Lord every day,
On you wilderness walk, not seeing your way.
Well, take heart cause it's all promised to you,
God will hone His Word and see your family through.

Like Joseph He'll set you on high with His Son,
He'll raise you up after you have done.
You appointed tune in the wilderness,
As you cling to your God and sin resist.

See those stories aren't so old for us today,
Take heart and let them encourage you on your way!
Mary agreed as soon as she had heard,
"Be it unto me according to thy word."

Dr. Lydia A. Woods

Just Said No

Daniel 3:1-30 (KJV)
Scripture Reference on page 158

I love that story in the Bible,
Of how the three Hebrew boys just said No.
Against the Kings final orders,
On their knees they would not go.

Not bow themselves down,
To that golden image that was made.
Even at the threat of death,
They would just have to go to the grave.

They had a confession of pure faith,
That even if God would not save,
They still believed in His power,
And the truth of His Word that He gave.

The most mighty men were called,
To throw them bound into the mist.
The mighty men were killed in the heat,
Shadrach, Meshach, and Abednego did not resist.

Under the Rainbow

As a matter of fact, it was told,
The king looked and saw four in the fire,
And One like unto the Son of God,
He was mighty quick to observe and admire.

The King called them from the mist of the fire,
To come out for they were not burned.
The King blessed the God of those boys,
The whole Kingdom was on that day turned.

For the decree was surely set up,
That every people, language, and nation,
That spoke anything against this true God,
Would suffer the ultimate humiliation.

They would be cut into many pieces,
And their house destroyed beyond repair,
 So "Just Say No," to the enemy,
Like the Hebrew boys – If You Dare!

Just Said No

Dr. Lydia A. Woods

She Was First

John 20:1-18; Luke 24:1-10; Mark 16:1-11; Matthew 28:1-8 (KJV)
Scripture Reference on page 159

Practically everyone knows her name,
Mentioned fourteen times to her fame.
Why this honor to a woman so,
There is something there that you should know.

That first day of the resurrection week,
Her slain Lord's body she did seek.
Mentioned first in every gospel book,
There is importance there – just have a look.

Jesus cast seven devils out of her you know,
From then on, she followed wherever He'd go.
She was faithful to the very end,
And for this faith – Honor she did win!

She was first to His tomb that glorious day,
She was first to hear the Angel say,
Why seek ye the living among the dead?
Go remind His disciples of what He said.

Under the Rainbow

That He would rise again on the third day,
She was first to see the Lord in the way.
The Lord called to her and spoke her name,
She answered "Rabonni" meaning master to the same.

She was not afraid to die for Him,
She stayed closer than His twelve friends.
She believed all that He had ever said,
She wept and mourned when He was dead.

She was first to know that He was alive,
She was first to run and testify,
She was first to have her joy fulfilled,
For her Lord had risen - He lived still.

This honor given to a woman with faith unseen,
She was first - this Mary Magdalene!

She Was First

Dr. Lydia A. Woods

So Be Like Job

Job 1:1, 8-12; 2:1-6; 42:12-13 (KJV)
Scripture Reference on page 163

Job was a mighty man of God they say,
He made offerings to God, every day.

He was perfect, upright, and very devout,
And God told Satan, to check him out.

His animals and beast were all carried away,
His servants were killed that terrible day.

A house it fell on his daughters and sons,
Only one was left, to tell all that was done.

Job ripped his clothes and was highly upset,
But he worshipped God, of that you can bet.

He blessed the name of the Lord and did not sin,
It sent Satan running back to the Lord again.

Under the Rainbow

This time Satan set out to do bodily harm,
He thought his next plan would work like a charm.

Job was cursed with sore boils on that day,
But he blessed his God, any old way.

Now even Job's wife pressed him the most,
To curse his God and give up the Ghost.

And even his friends tried to cause him to sin,
But he was full of the Spirit and he did win,

Cause the Latter End of Job was truly blessed,
For the faith and trust he did possess.

So be like job in your steadfast Love,
And receive your blessings from God above.

So Be Like Job

Chapter 7 –
The Movies:
Their Spiritual Messages

The Circle of Life 87
E.T. 89
If You Build It 91
May the Force... 93
The Mummy's Curse 94
The Red Pill or the Blue 95
The Richest Man in Town 97

Dr. Lydia A. Woods

The Circle of Life

Genesis 4:1-11; 33:4,10-11 (KJV)
Scripture Reference on page 166
Movie – "The Lion King"

Simba was the son of the Lion King,
This was a proud and wonderful thing.

There was one who hoped he had never been born,
His Uncle Scar, looked at his birth with scorn.

On Simba's birth, Scar plotted his throne to take,
To kill the King and his son – make no mistake.

Scar wanted power and respect so his brother he killed,
Like Cain and Abel evil continues still.

Simba ran away out of guilt and shame,
Leaving his birthright to evil he dishonored his name.

Years later Simba was reminded of his precious birthright,
Went back to face evil and give him a fight.

The truth and love that was in his heart,
Overthrew evil and restore him to his rightful part.

In the end the One True King stood with his son and wife,
And so the story continues unbroken – the Circle of Life!

𝓔.𝓣.

John 14:1-4 (KJV)
Scripture Reference on page 168
Movie – "E.T. – The Extraterrestrial"

You've all seen the movie,
But what you didn't see,
Is that E.T. looks,
A lot like you and me.

Now he was left on earth,
By those he loved,
And he searched for their return
In the heavens above.

I'm sure he volunteered,
To be part of the crew,
To complete the task,
That they came to earth to do.

But the job got a little complex,
And scary towards the end,
He didn't bargain for all the trouble,
That befell him.

Phone home E. T.,
So your people will know,
That you have had enough of earth,
And you are ready to go!

They pursued you and sought,
To take your life,
Why did they leave you here
With all this strife?

Under the Rainbow

What lessons have you learned,
In your brief stay,
You met some gentle and loving people,
Along the way.

But what about those others,
Who were full of fear,
Because of your difference,
You became a threat here.

But you left your mark,
And touched some souls,
You showed them love,
The young and the old.

Your purpose completed,
They did come back for you,
And you were changed,
By this earthly experience too.

The spiritual message in that film,
Speaks to you and me,
For this strange place earth,
Is grievous you see.

Lord I identify with E. T.,
And long to be,
Back home with You,
In Eternity!

E.T.

Dr. Lydia A. Woods

If You Build It

**1 Samuel 15:22; Hebrews 11:6; John 10:27; Philippians 2:13;
Ephesians 1:9 (KJV) Scripture Reference on page 169
Movie – "The Field of Dreams"**

I must admit I am hooked for sure,
The "Field of Dreams," movie is my cure.
It's just like a good old friend,
That I call on the phone every now and then.

I love it when Ray hears the "Voice,"
And he is commanded and has no choice.
"If You Build it He will Come,"
Of course was foolishness to some.

A Baseball field in the middle of his corn,
Is foolishness to any farmer born.
But when the "Voice" speaks what can you do,
But His bidding as He's commanded you.

To others you will look quite odd,
It's what happens when you hear the voice of God.
Are you ready to risk it all?
When you respond to His call.

Then he was told to, "Go the Distance,"
That's what you get when you listen,
You responded to the first call that's fine,
Now the second call plays with your mind.

Under the Rainbow

Where is this thing going - what else must I do,
And for a time you won't even have a clue.
It takes greater faith the second time round,
But you won't let fear pull you down.

"Ease his pain," Now come on what does that mean,
This is becoming a really crazy thing.
I have done all that you command,
Now I really just don't understand.

What's in it for me?" was Ray's plea.
In all I have done your purpose I can't see.
Then when finally, it is all revealed,
You feel awfully low just like a real heel.

For the Blessing is filled with tremendous Love,
How could we ever doubt the Holy One above.
Obedience delivers us from our own grievous pain,
And it is the victory that we can finally claim!

Dr. Lydia A. Woods

May the Force...

1 Corinthians 13:4-7 (KJV)
Scripture Reference on page 170
Movie – "Star Wars"

May the "Force be with you" – is now a famous line,
Used in the "Star Wars" movies in a future time.

The power of the "Force" is fueled by Love,
And the source of Love comes from the Father above.

The Emperor represents the "Dark Side," for sure,
Charged by evil – enemy to those who are pure.

Evil will always be overcome by Love – that's a fact,
And rebel forces used the "Force" to make a counterattack.

The "Dark Side" can seduce with power and greed,
Flourish in an evil heart like a rotten seed.

Vader cast his alliance with the Emperor for power,
But the Emperor's plan to get Luke too – went sour.

The "Force" was strong in Luke's family – that's true,
His father had it, and his father's father too.

Luke used the "Force" not his natural sight,
To destroy the "death star" during that final flight.

He used the "Force" to overcome his father's sins,
With Love, pulled Darth Vader from the "Dark Side" in the end.

May the "Force" be strong in your family, as well,
And let the "Force" guide your feet from the path of hell!

The Mummy's Curse

Romans 6:6-7 (KJV)
Scripture Reference on page 171
Movie – "The Mummy"

The mummy rests within His tomb,
Disturb Him at the risk of doom.
There is always a mummy's curse,
At the risk of death or even worse.

And there is always that unsuspecting soul,
In search of the mummy's gold.
And then they make that fatal mistake.
As the mummy's gold they attempt to take.

Well, that "old man" in you and me,
Is like the mummy never really dead you see.
He can be disturbed at any time.
And come alive to commit evil crimes.

And your old man his flesh all rotten
In death has not really forgotten.
How the fleshly works succeed,
To destroy us with its sinful deeds.

So, keep the mummy in his tomb today,
Make sure that old man is locked away.
My advice is to run - that's what you do,
So, the next victim of the mummy won't be you!

Dr. Lydia A. Woods

The Red Pill or the Blue

John 10:10; Romans 12:2-3; Proverbs 9:10 (KJV)
Scripture Reference on page 172
Movie – "The Matrix"

Reality – I'm afraid there is something you should know,
Look around you it's not real – in the Matrix it was so.

The real world you cannot see with the naked eye,
Illusion and delusion and here's the reason why.

Neo wasn't really ready to handle the truth,
But he took the red pill and they provided him the proof.

He entered a world that was positively strange,
All the time under the surface just outside the brain.

From the knowledge of truth there is no turning back,
Neo's feet were firmly planted on that final track.

Join the fight become a solider for the war is just begun,
You are fighting for your life but Neo he was the One.

Predicted by the Oracle – now the fight could be won,
Morpheus knew in his heart that Neo was the One.

Slowly Neo got the message he was chosen from the start,
He had only to step up take his place and do his part.

Under the Rainbow

To save them all from darkness a world they could not see,
And defeat the enemy to make the world safe and free.

Of course, you see where I'm going – I know you get my drift,
Because just like Neo we are chosen with that special gift.

The gift to become sons and daughters of God,
Taking our position in a world that thinks us odd.

Now that you know of the illusion and what is real,
You don't care about this life – it's about the eternal deal.

You have gifts and powers to defeat the enemy in your face,
Using weapons not known to the world given by His grace.

Weapons and powers that the world does not know,
Jesus the Savior left it just so.

The Matrix is constructed by the enemy to keep you blind,
Stealing your life little by little by darkening your mind.

So, take the red pill today never regret what you have picked,
And join us in the fight to destroy the Matrix!

The Red Pill or the Blue

Dr. Lydia A. Woods

The Richest Man in Town

John 15:13; Matthew 6:19; Proverbs 18:22; Psalms 91:11 (KJV)
Scripture Reference on page 173
Movie – "It's a Wonderful Life"

George found out that he had a wonderful life,
Changed many a life – had four children and a good wife.

He didn't fulfill his dreams of traveling the world,
Didn't go to college – But got his favorite girl.

He lived all of his life in that small little town,
Making a difference in every life – no better man could be found.

He lived a life of usefulness, self-sacrifice and good,
But he didn't appreciate it fully as he should.

His frustrations built – he wanted to end it all,
As he stood on the bridge facing that fatal fall.

But he jumped in to save one who cried out for help,
And in doing so answered his prayer for himself.

Clarence, the Angel from heaven showed him the way,
Back to his family and friends on that fateful day.

"Every time a bell rings an Angel gets his wings,"
Angels are the servants of the children of the King.

Under the Rainbow

They bear them up lest they dash their foot upon a stone,
Always standing near from birth till you are full-grown.

Mr. Potter was the one used for evil in the film,
To destroy the good in George and push him to the rim.

There are many Mr. Potter's in everyone's life,
Used to kill, steal, and destroy through frustration and strife.

But God had a plan for George – like all of us,
And frustration builds when we lack trust.

In the Father's purpose to use our life for good,
And how blessed we are when this purpose is understood.

He didn't live in a fancy house – not much money – you know,
He thought his life a waste with nothing to show,

And in the final scene Clarence reminded him,
"That no man is a failure when he has friends."

"A toast to my brother George," – You could not hear a sound,
As everyone raised their glass – to the Richest Man in Town!

The Richest Man in Town

Scriptural References

Chapter 1 -
The Father, Son, and Holy Spirit

Ain't He All That! 102
He's Good At 103
Master of Masters 105
Pieces of Myself 108
Somethin' Told Me 109
That Small Still Voice 110
With His Own Blood 111

Ain't He All That!

Hebrews 1:2-3; John 1:1-5; Revelation 22:13 (KJV)

Hebrews 1:2-3 (KJV)
2 Hath in these last days spoken unto us by his Son, whom he hath appointed heir of all things, by whom also he made the worlds;
3 Who being the brightness of his glory, and the express image of his person, and upholding all things by the word of his power, when he had by himself purged our sins, sat down on the right hand of the Majesty on high:

John 1:1-5 (KJV)
1 In the beginning was the Word, and the Word was with God, and the Word was God.
2 The same was in the beginning with God.
3 All things were made by him; and without him was not anything made that was made.
4 In him was life; and the life was the light of men.
5 And the light shineth in darkness; and the darkness comprehended it not.

Revelation 22:13 (KJV)
13 I am Alpha and Omega, the beginning and the end, the first and the last.

Dr. Lydia A. Woods

𝓗𝑒'𝑠 𝓖𝑜𝑜𝑑 𝓐𝑡

Genesis 1:3, 9, 12, 16, 24, 27, 31; Isaiah 14:27, 46:9-11 (KJV)

Genesis 1:3 (KJV)
3 And God said, Let there be light: and there was light.

Genesis 1:9 (KJV)
9 And God said, Let the waters under the heaven be gathered together unto one place, and let the dry land appear: and it was so.

Genesis 1:12 (KJV)
12 And the earth brought forth grass, and herb yielding seed after his kind, and the tree yielding fruit, whose seed was in itself, after his kind: and God saw that it was good.

Genesis 1:16 (KJV)
16 And God made two great lights; the greater light to rule the day, and the lesser light to rule the night: he made the stars also.

Genesis 1:24 (KJV)
24 And God said, Let the earth bring forth the living creature after his kind, cattle, and creeping thing, and beast of the earth after his kind: and it was so.

Genesis 1:27 (KJV)
27 So God created man in his own image, in the image of God created he him; male and female created he them.

Genesis 1:31 (KJV)
27 And God saw every thing that he had made, and, behold, it was very good. And the evening and the morning were the sixth day.

Isaiah 14:27 (KJV)
27 For the Lord of hosts hath purposed, and who shall disannul it? and his hand is stretched out, and who shall turn it back?

Isaiah 46:9-11 (KJV)

⁹ Remember the former things of old: for I am God, and there is none else; I am God, and there is none like me,
¹⁰ Declaring the end from the beginning, and from ancient times the things that are not yet done, saying, My counsel shall stand, and I will do all my pleasure:
¹¹ Calling a ravenous bird from the east, the man that executeth my counsel from a far country: yea, I have spoken it, I will also bring it to pass; I have purposed it, I will also do it.

Dr. Lydia A. Woods

Master of Masters

Matthew 4:1, 4:19, 5:1, 7:29, 8:26, 11:5; Luke 8:43-48;
John 2:1-11, 11:43-44 (KJV)

Matthew 4:1 (KJV)
¹ Then was Jesus led up of the Spirit into the wilderness to be tempted of the devil.

Matthew 4:19 (KJV)
¹⁹ And he saith unto them, Follow me, and I will make you fishers of men.

Matthew 5:1 (KJV)
¹ And seeing the multitudes, he went up into a mountain: and when he was set, his disciples came unto him:

Matthew 7:29 (KJV)
²⁹ For he taught them as one having authority, and not as the scribes.

Matthew 8:26 (KJV)
²⁶ And he saith unto them, Why are ye fearful, O ye of little faith? Then he arose, and rebuked the winds and the sea; and there was a great calm.

Matthew 11:5 (KJV)
⁵ The blind receive their sight, and the lame walk, the lepers are cleansed, and the deaf hear, the dead are raised up, and the poor have the gospel preached to them.

Luke 8:43-48 (KJV)
⁴³ And a woman having an issue of blood twelve years, which had spent all her living upon physicians, neither could be healed of any,
⁴⁴ Came behind him, and touched the border of his garment: and immediately her issue of blood stanched.
⁴⁵ And Jesus said, Who touched me? When all denied, Peter and they that were with him said, Master, the multitude throng thee and press thee, and sayest thou, Who touched me?

⁴⁶ And Jesus said, Somebody hath touched me: for I perceive that virtue is gone out of me.

⁴⁷ And when the woman saw that she was not hid, she came trembling, and falling down before him, she declared unto him before all the people for what cause she had touched him, and how she was healed immediately.

⁴⁸ And he said unto her, Daughter, be of good comfort: thy faith hath made thee whole; go in peace.

John 2:1-11 (KJV)

¹ And the third day there was a marriage in Cana of Galilee; and the mother of Jesus was there:

² And both Jesus was called, and his disciples, to the marriage.

³ And when they wanted wine, the mother of Jesus saith unto him, They have no wine.

⁴ Jesus saith unto her, Woman, what have I to do with thee? mine hour is not yet come.

⁵ His mother saith unto the servants, Whatsoever he saith unto you, do it.

⁶ And there were set there six waterpots of stone, after the manner of the purifying of the Jews, containing two or three firkins apiece.

⁷ Jesus saith unto them, Fill the waterpots with water. And they filled them up to the brim.

⁸ And he saith unto them, Draw out now, and bear unto the governor of the feast. And they bare it.

⁹ When the ruler of the feast had tasted the water that was made wine, and knew not whence it was: (but the servants which drew the water knew;) the governor of the feast called the bridegroom,

¹⁰ And saith unto him, Every man at the beginning doth set forth good wine; and when men have well drunk, then that which is worse: but thou hast kept the good wine until now.
¹¹ This beginning of miracles did Jesus in Cana of Galilee, and manifested forth his glory; and his disciples believed on him.

John 11:43-44 (KJV)
⁴³ And when he thus had spoken, he cried with a loud voice, Lazarus, come forth.
⁴⁴ And he that was dead came forth, bound hand and foot with graveclothes: and his face was bound about with a napkin. Jesus saith unto them, Loose him, and let him go.

Pieces of Myself

Hebrews 13:5; Romans 12:3; Ephesians 4:7 (KJV)

Hebrews 13:5 (KJV)
⁵ Let your conversation be without covetousness; and be content with such things as ye have: for he hath said, I will never leave thee, nor forsake thee.

Romans 12:3 (KJV)
³ For I say, through the grace given unto me, to every man that is among you, not to think of himself more highly than he ought to think; but to think soberly, according as God hath dealt to every man the measure of faith.

Ephesians 4:7 (KJV)
⁷ But unto every one of us is given grace according to the measure of the gift of Christ.

Dr. Lydia A. Woods

Somethin' Told Me

John 12:26; Ephesians 4:30; Luke 2:26 (KJV)

John 12:26 (KJV)
[26] If any man serve me, let him follow me; and where I am, there shall also my servant be: if any man serve me, him will my Father honour.

Ephesians 4:30 (KJV)
[30] And grieve not the holy Spirit of God, whereby ye are sealed unto the day of redemption.

Luke 2:26 (KJV)
[26] And it was revealed unto him by the Holy Ghost, that he should not see death, before he had seen the Lord's Christ.

That Small Still Voice

Psalms 95:7; Hebrews 3:7 (KJV)

Psalms 95:7 (KJV)
⁷ For he is our God; and we are the people of his pasture, and the sheep of his hand. To day if ye will hear his voice,

Hebrews 3:7 (KJV)
⁷ Wherefore (as the Holy Ghost saith, To day if ye will hear his voice,

Dr. Lydia A. Woods

With His Own Blood

Acts 20:28; Hosea 2:19; Revelation 19:7-9;21:9 (KJV)

Acts 20:28 (KJV)
28 Take heed therefore unto yourselves, and to all the flock, over the which the Holy Ghost hath made you overseers, to feed the church of God, which he hath purchased with his own blood.

Hosea 2:19 (KJV)
19 And I will betroth thee unto me for ever; yea, I will betroth thee unto me in righteousness, and in judgment, and in lovingkindness, and in mercies.

Revelation 19:7-9 (KJV)
7 Let us be glad and rejoice, and give honour to him: for the marriage of the Lamb is come, and his wife hath made herself ready.
8 And to her was granted that she should be arrayed in fine linen, clean and white: for the fine linen is the righteousness of saints.
9 And he saith unto me, Write, Blessed are they which are called unto the marriage supper of the Lamb. And he saith unto me, These are the true sayings of God.

Revelation 21:9 (KJV)
9 And there came unto me one of the seven angels which had the seven vials full of the seven last plagues, and talked with me, saying, Come hither, I will shew thee the bride, the Lamb's wife.

Chapter 2 - Finding Out Who You Are

A Bible Character 113
The Brightest Light 116
If Thou Be... 117
I'm Not Lucky – I'm Blessed 118
It is Your Destiny 120
Scariest Journey 121
Simply Because You Are Mine 122

Dr. Lydia A. Woods

A Bible Character

Luke 22:47, 57, 60; 23:21-34; Mark 15:1, 10-11; 16:1; Matthew 21:24; 1 Peter 2:9 (KJV)

Luke 22:47 (KJV)
47 And while he yet spake, behold a multitude, and he that was called Judas, one of the twelve, went before them, and drew near unto Jesus to kiss him.

Luke 22:57 (KJV)
57 And he denied him, saying, Woman, I know him not.

Luke 22:60 (KJV)
60 And Peter said, Man, I know not what thou sayest. And immediately, while he yet spake, the cock crew.

Luke 23:21-34 (KJV)
21 But they cried, saying, Crucify him, crucify him.
22 And he said unto them the third time, Why, what evil hath he done? I have found no cause of death in him: I will therefore chastise him, and let him go.
23 And they were instant with loud voices, requiring that he might be crucified. And the voices of them and of the chief priests prevailed.
24 And Pilate gave sentence that it should be as they required.
25 And he released unto them him that for sedition and murder was cast into prison, whom they had desired; but he delivered Jesus to their will.
26 And as they led him away, they laid hold upon one Simon, a Cyrenian, coming out of the country, and on him they laid the cross, that he might bear it after Jesus.
27 And there followed him a great company of people, and of women, which also bewailed and lamented him.
28 But Jesus turning unto them said, Daughters of Jerusalem, weep not for me, but weep for yourselves, and for your children.

²⁹ For, behold, the days are coming, in the which they shall say, Blessed are the barren, and the wombs that never bare, and the paps which never gave suck.
³⁰ Then shall they begin to say to the mountains, Fall on us; and to the hills, Cover us.
³¹ For if they do these things in a green tree, what shall be done in the dry?
³² And there were also two other, malefactors, led with him to be put to death.
³³ And when they were come to the place, which is called Calvary, there they crucified him, and the malefactors, one on the right hand, and the other on the left.
³⁴ Then said Jesus, Father, forgive them; for they know not what they do. And they parted his raiment, and cast lots.

Mark 15:1 (KJV)
¹ And straightway in the morning the chief priests held a consultation with the elders and scribes and the whole council, and bound Jesus, and carried him away, and delivered him to Pilate.

Mark 15:10-11 (KJV)
¹⁰ For he knew that the chief priests had delivered him for envy.
¹¹ But the chief priests moved the people, that he should rather release Barabbas unto them.

Mark 16:1 (KJV)
¹ And when the sabbath was past, Mary Magdalene, and Mary the mother of James, and Salome, had bought sweet spices, that they might come and anoint him.

Matthew 21:24 (KJV)

²⁴ And Jesus answered and said unto them, I also will ask you one thing, which if ye tell me, I in like wise will tell you by what authority I do these things.

1 Peter 2:9 (KJV)
⁹ But ye are a chosen generation, a royal priesthood, an holy nation, a peculiar people; that ye should shew forth the praises of him who hath called you out of darkness into his marvellous light;

The Brightest Light

Matthew 5:14-16 (KJV)

Matthew 5:14-16 (KJV)
[14] Ye are the light of the world. A city that is set on an hill cannot be hid.
[15] Neither do men light a candle, and put it under a bushel, but on a candlestick; and it giveth light unto all that are in the house.
[16] Let your light so shine before men, that they may see your good works, and glorify your Father which is in heaven.

If Thou Be...

Luke 4:1-13 (KJV)

Luke 4:1-13 (KJV)
[1] And Jesus being full of the Holy Ghost returned from Jordan, and was led by the Spirit into the wilderness,
[2] Being forty days tempted of the devil. And in those days he did eat nothing: and when they were ended, he afterward hungered.
[3] And the devil said unto him, If thou be the Son of God, command this stone that it be made bread.
[4] And Jesus answered him, saying, It is written, That man shall not live by bread alone, but by every word of God.
[5] And the devil, taking him up into an high mountain, shewed unto him all the kingdoms of the world in a moment of time.
[6] And the devil said unto him, All this power will I give thee, and the glory of them: for that is delivered unto me; and to whomsoever I will I give it.
[7] If thou therefore wilt worship me, all shall be thine.
[8] And Jesus answered and said unto him, Get thee behind me, Satan: for it is written, Thou shalt worship the Lord thy God, and him only shalt thou serve.
[9] And he brought him to Jerusalem, and set him on a pinnacle of the temple, and said unto him, If thou be the Son of God, cast thyself down from hence:
[10] For it is written, He shall give his angels charge over thee, to keep thee:
[11] And in their hands they shall bear thee up, lest at any time thou dash thy foot against a stone.
[12] And Jesus answering said unto him, It is said, Thou shalt not tempt the Lord thy God.
[13] And when the devil had ended all the temptation, he departed from him for a season.

I'm Not Lucky - I'm Blessed

Genesis 12:3, 26:4; Deuteronomy 7:3-14 (KJV)

Genesis 12:3 (KJV)
3 And I will bless them that bless thee, and curse him that curseth thee: and in thee shall all families of the earth be blessed.

Genesis 26:4 (KJV)
4 And I will make thy seed to multiply as the stars of heaven, and will give unto thy seed all these countries; and in thy seed shall all the nations of the earth be blessed;

Deuteronomy 7:3-14 (KJV)
3 Neither shalt thou make marriages with them; thy daughter thou shalt not give unto his son, nor his daughter shalt thou take unto thy son.
4 For they will turn away thy son from following me, that they may serve other gods: so will the anger of the Lord be kindled against you, and destroy thee suddenly.
5 But thus shall ye deal with them; ye shall destroy their altars, and break down their images, and cut down their groves, and burn their graven images with fire.
6 For thou art an holy people unto the Lord thy God: the Lord thy God hath chosen thee to be a special people unto himself, above all people that are upon the face of the earth.
7 The Lord did not set his love upon you, nor choose you, because ye were more in number than any people; for ye were the fewest of all people:
8 But because the Lord loved you, and because he would keep the oath which he had sworn unto your fathers, hath the Lord brought you out with a mighty hand, and redeemed you out of the house of bondmen, from the hand of Pharaoh king of Egypt.

⁹ Know therefore that the Lord thy God, he is God, the faithful God, which keepeth covenant and mercy with them that love him and keep his commandments to a thousand generations;

¹⁰ And repayeth them that hate him to their face, to destroy them: he will not be slack to him that hateth him, he will repay him to his face.

¹¹ Thou shalt therefore keep the commandments, and the statutes, and the judgments, which I command thee this day, to do them.

¹² Wherefore it shall come to pass, if ye hearken to these judgments, and keep, and do them, that the Lord thy God shall keep unto thee the covenant and the mercy which he sware unto thy fathers:

¹³ And he will love thee, and bless thee, and multiply thee: he will also bless the fruit of thy womb, and the fruit of thy land, thy corn, and thy wine, and thine oil, the increase of thy kine, and the flocks of thy sheep, in the land which he sware unto thy fathers to give thee.

¹⁴ Thou shalt be blessed above all people: there shall not be male or female barren among you, or among your cattle.

It is Your Destiny

Psalms 139:1-6; 14-18 (KJV)

Psalms 139:1-6 (KJV)
[1] O lord, thou hast searched me, and known me.
[2] Thou knowest my downsitting and mine uprising, thou understandest my thought afar off.
[3] Thou compassest my path and my lying down, and art acquainted with all my ways.
[4] For there is not a word in my tongue, but, lo, O Lord, thou knowest it altogether.
[5] Thou hast beset me behind and before, and laid thine hand upon me.
[6] Such knowledge is too wonderful for me; it is high, I cannot attain unto it.

Psalms 139:14-18 (KJV)
[14] I will praise thee; for I am fearfully and wonderfully made: marvellous are thy works; and that my soul knoweth right well.
[15] My substance was not hid from thee, when I was made in secret, and curiously wrought in the lowest parts of the earth.
[16] Thine eyes did see my substance, yet being unperfect; and in thy book all my members were written, which in continuance were fashioned, when as yet there was none of them.
[17] How precious also are thy thoughts unto me, O God! how great is the sum of them!
[18] If I should count them, they are more in number than the sand: when I awake, I am still with thee.

Dr. Lydia A. Woods

Scariest Journey

Luke 17:21; John 14:6 (KJV)

Luke 17:21 (KJV)
[21] Neither shall they say, Lo here! or, lo there! for, behold, the kingdom of God is within you.

John 14:6 (KJV)
[6] Jesus saith unto him, I am the way, the truth, and the life: no man cometh unto the Father, but by me.

Scripture References

Simply Because You Are Mine

Matthew 7:11; 1 Corinthians 2:9-11; Isaiah 64:4; Psalms 31:19 (KJV)

Matthew 7:11 (KJV)
11 If ye then, being evil, know how to give good gifts unto your children, how much more shall your Father which is in heaven give good things to them that ask him?

1 Corinthians 2:9-11 (KJV)
9 But as it is written, Eye hath not seen, nor ear heard, neither have entered into the heart of man, the things which God hath prepared for them that love him.

10 But God hath revealed them unto us by his Spirit: for the Spirit searcheth all things, yea, the deep things of God.

11 For what man knoweth the things of a man, save the spirit of man which is in him? even so the things of God knoweth no man, but the Spirit of God.

Isaiah 64:4 (KJV)
4 For since the beginning of the world men have not heard, nor perceived by the ear, neither hath the eye seen, O God, beside thee, what he hath prepared for him that waiteth for him.

Psalms 31:19 (KJV)
19 Oh how great is thy goodness, which thou hast laid up for them that fear thee; which thou hast wrought for them that trust in thee before the sons of men!

Chapter 3 – Encouragement

Be Not Afraid, Only Believe 124
Be Still! 125
Good News 126
Happy is the Woman or Man 128
Hero in You 130
It's Alright 131
Your Gifts and Talents 132

Be Not Afraid, Only Believe

Mark 5:35-43 (KJV)

Mark 5:35-43 (KJV)

35 While he yet spake, there came from the ruler of the synagogue's house certain which said, Thy daughter is dead: why troublest thou the Master any further?

36 As soon as Jesus heard the word that was spoken, he saith unto the ruler of the synagogue, Be not afraid, only believe.

37 And he suffered no man to follow him, save Peter, and James, and John the brother of James.

38 And he cometh to the house of the ruler of the synagogue, and seeth the tumult, and them that wept and wailed greatly.

39 And when he was come in, he saith unto them, Why make ye this ado, and weep? the damsel is not dead, but sleepeth.

40 And they laughed him to scorn. But when he had put them all out, he taketh the father and the mother of the damsel, and them that were with him, and entereth in where the damsel was lying.

41 And he took the damsel by the hand, and said unto her, Talitha cumi; which is, being interpreted, Damsel, I say unto thee, arise.

42 And straightway the damsel arose, and walked; for she was of the age of twelve years. And they were astonished with a great astonishment.

43 And he charged them straitly that no man should know it; and commanded that something should be given her to eat.

Be Still!

Psalms 46:10 (KJV)

Psalms 46:10 (KJV)
[10] Be still, and know that I am God: I will be exalted among the heathen, I will be exalted in the earth.

Good News

1 Corinthians 15:3, 15:52; Mark 13:24-27; Revelation 1:7, 19:7-9, 20:1-3, 21:1-5 (KJV)

1 Corinthians 15:3 (KJV)
3 For I delivered unto you first of all that which I also received, how that Christ died for our sins according to the scriptures;

1 Corinthians 15:52 (KJV)
52 In a moment, in the twinkling of an eye, at the last trump: for the trumpet shall sound, and the dead shall be raised incorruptible, and we shall be changed.

Mark 13:24-27 (KJV)
24 But in those days, after that tribulation, the sun shall be darkened, and the moon shall not give her light,
25 And the stars of heaven shall fall, and the powers that are in heaven shall be shaken.
26 And then shall they see the Son of man coming in the clouds with great power and glory.
27 And then shall he send his angels, and shall gather together his elect from the four winds, from the uttermost part of the earth to the uttermost part of heaven.

Revelation 1:7 (KJV)
7 Behold, he cometh with clouds; and every eye shall see him, and they also which pierced him: and all kindreds of the earth shall wail because of him. Even so, Amen.

Revelation 19:7-9 (KJV)
7 Let us be glad and rejoice, and give honour to him: for the marriage of the Lamb is come, and his wife hath made herself ready.
8 And to her was granted that she should be arrayed in fine linen, clean and white: for the fine linen is the righteousness of saints.

⁹ And he saith unto me, Write, Blessed are they which are called unto the marriage supper of the Lamb. And he saith unto me, These are the true sayings of God.

Revelation 20:1-3 (KJV)
¹ And I saw an angel come down from heaven, having the key of the bottomless pit and a great chain in his hand.
² And he laid hold on the dragon, that old serpent, which is the Devil, and Satan, and bound him a thousand years,
³ And cast him into the bottomless pit, and shut him up, and set a seal upon him, that he should deceive the nations no more, till the thousand years should be fulfilled: and after that he must be loosed a little season.

Revelation 21:1-5 (KJV)
¹ And I saw a new heaven and a new earth: for the first heaven and the first earth were passed away; and there was no more sea.
² And I John saw the holy city, new Jerusalem, coming down from God out of heaven, prepared as a bride adorned for her husband.
³ And I heard a great voice out of heaven saying, Behold, the tabernacle of God is with men, and he will dwell with them, and they shall be his people, and God himself shall be with them, and be their God.
⁴ And God shall wipe away all tears from their eyes; and there shall be no more death, neither sorrow, nor crying, neither shall there be any more pain: for the former things are passed away.
⁵ And he that sat upon the throne said, Behold, I make all things new. And he said unto me, Write: for these words are true and faithful.

Happy is the Woman or Man

Proverbs 3:1-18 (KJV)

Proverbs 3:1-18 (KJV)

[1] My son, forget not my law; but let thine heart keep my commandments:

[2] For length of days, and long life, and peace, shall they add to thee.

[3] Let not mercy and truth forsake thee: bind them about thy neck; write them upon the table of thine heart:

[4] So shalt thou find favour and good understanding in the sight of God and man.

[5] Trust in the Lord with all thine heart; and lean not unto thine own understanding.

[6] In all thy ways acknowledge him, and he shall direct thy paths.

[7] Be not wise in thine own eyes: fear the Lord, and depart from evil.

[8] It shall be health to thy navel, and marrow to thy bones.

[9] Honour the Lord with thy substance, and with the firstfruits of all thine increase:

[10] So shall thy barns be filled with plenty, and thy presses shall burst out with new wine.

[11] My son, despise not the chastening of the Lord; neither be weary of his correction:

[12] For whom the Lord loveth he correcteth; even as a father the son in whom he delighteth.

[13] Happy is the man that findeth wisdom, and the man that getteth understanding.

[14] For the merchandise of it is better than the merchandise of silver, and the gain thereof than fine gold.

[15] She is more precious than rubies: and all the things thou canst desire are not to be compared unto her.

[16] Length of days is in her right hand; and in her left hand riches and honour.

[17] Her ways are ways of pleasantness, and all her paths are peace.

¹⁸ She is a tree of life to them that lay hold upon her: and happy is every one that retaineth her.

Hero in You

John 15:13 (KJV)

John 15:13 (KJV)
[13] Greater love hath no man than this, that a man lay down his life for his friends.

Dr. Lydia A. Woods

It's Alright
James 1:5 (KJV)

James 1:5 (KJV)
5 If any of you lack wisdom, let him ask of God, that giveth to all men liberally, and upbraideth not; and it shall be given him.

Your Gifts and Talents

Job 33:6; Isaiah 29:16; 45:9; 64:8; Matthew 6:10; 25:45 (KJV)

Job 33:6 (KJV)
6 Behold, I am according to thy wish in God's stead: I also am formed out of the clay.

Isaiah 29:16 (KJV)
16 Surely your turning of things upside down shall be esteemed as the potter's clay: for shall the work say of him that made it, He made me not? or shall the thing framed say of him that framed it, He had no understanding?

Isaiah 45:9 (KJV)
9 Woe unto him that striveth with his Maker! Let the potsherd strive with the potsherds of the earth. Shall the clay say to him that fashioneth it, What makest thou? or thy work, He hath no hands?

Isaiah 64:8 (KJV)
8 But now, O Lord, thou art our father; we are the clay, and thou our potter; and we all are the work of thy hand.

Matthew 6:10 (KJV)
10 Thy kingdom come, Thy will be done in earth, as it is in heaven.

Matthew 25:45 (KJV)
45 Then shall he answer them, saying, Verily I say unto you, Inasmuch as ye did it not to one of the least of these, ye did it not to me.

Chapter 4 –
Words of Advice

Back Talk 134
Doin' the Israelite 135
Forgive or Forgive Not 137
Garbage in Garbage Out! 138
If You Want To Make God Laugh! 139
Lean Not 140
Love is An Action 141

Back Talk

Ephesians 2:2; 2 Chronicles 30:8; 1 Peter 1:2 (KJV)

Ephesians 2:2 (KJV)
2 Wherein in time past ye walked according to the course of this world, according to the prince of the power of the air, the spirit that now worketh in the children of disobedience:

2 Chronicles 30:8 (KJV)
8 Now be ye not stiffnecked, as your fathers were, but yield yourselves unto the Lord, and enter into his sanctuary, which he hath sanctified for ever: and serve the Lord your God, that the fierceness of his wrath may turn away from you.

1 Peter 1:2 (KJV)
2 Elect according to the foreknowledge of God the Father, through sanctification of the Spirit, unto obedience and sprinkling of the blood of Jesus Christ: Grace unto you, and peace, be multiplied.

Dr. Lydia A. Woods

Doin' the Israelite

Exodus 11:2; 13:21; 14:27-28; 16:2-3,12; 17:2-4 (KJV)

Exodus 11:2 (KJV)
2 Speak now in the ears of the people, and let every man borrow of his neighbour, and every woman of her neighbour, jewels of silver and jewels of gold.

Exodus 13:21 (KJV)
21 And the Lord went before them by day in a pillar of a cloud, to lead them the way; and by night in a pillar of fire, to give them light; to go by day and night:

Exodus 14:27-28 (KJV)
27 And Moses stretched forth his hand over the sea, and the sea returned to his strength when the morning appeared; and the Egyptians fled against it; and the Lord overthrew the Egyptians in the midst of the sea.

28 And the waters returned, and covered the chariots, and the horsemen, and all the host of Pharaoh that came into the sea after them; there remained not so much as one of them.

Exodus 16:2-3 (KJV)
2 And the whole congregation of the children of Israel murmured against Moses and Aaron in the wilderness:

3 And the children of Israel said unto them, Would to God we had died by the hand of the Lord in the land of Egypt, when we sat by the flesh pots, and when we did eat bread to the full; for ye have brought us forth into this wilderness, to kill this whole assembly with hunger.

Exodus 16:12 (KJV)
12 I have heard the murmurings of the children of Israel: speak unto them, saying, At even ye shall eat flesh, and in the morning ye shall be filled with bread; and ye shall know that I am the Lord your God.

Exodus 17:2-4 (KJV)

2 Wherefore the people did chide with Moses, and said, Give us water that we may drink. And Moses said unto them, Why chide ye with me? wherefore do ye tempt the Lord?

3 And the people thirsted there for water; and the people murmured against Moses, and said, Wherefore is this that thou hast brought us up out of Egypt, to kill us and our children and our cattle with thirst?

4 And Moses cried unto the Lord, saying, What shall I do unto this people? they be almost ready to stone me.

Dr. Lydia A. Woods

Forgive or Forgive Not

Luke 6:37; Mark 11:25-26 (KJV)

Luke 6:37 (KJV)
37 Judge not, and ye shall not be judged: condemn not, and ye shall not be condemned: forgive, and ye shall be forgiven:

Mark 11:25-26 (KJV)
25 And when ye stand praying, forgive, if ye have ought against any: that your Father also which is in heaven may forgive you your trespasses.
26 But if ye do not forgive, neither will your Father which is in heaven forgive your trespasses.

Garbage in Garbage Out!

Philippians 4:8-9 (KJV)

Philippians 4:8-9 (KJV)

[8] Finally, brethren, whatsoever things are true, whatsoever things are honest, whatsoever things are just, whatsoever things are pure, whatsoever things are lovely, whatsoever things are of good report; if there be any virtue, and if there be any praise, think on these things. [9] Those things, which ye have both learned, and received, and heard, and seen in me, do: and the God of peace shall be with you.

Dr. Lydia A. Woods

If You Want To Make God Laugh!

Proverbs 19:21; Matthew 5:36; Isaiah 46:9-11 (KJV)

Proverbs 19:21 (KJV)
[21] There are many devices in a man's heart; nevertheless the counsel of the Lord, that shall stand.

Matthew 5:36 (KJV)
[36] Neither shalt thou swear by thy head, because thou canst not make one hair white or black.

Isaiah 46:9-11 (KJV)
[9] Remember the former things of old: for I am God, and there is none else; I am God, and there is none like me,
[10] Declaring the end from the beginning, and from ancient times the things that are not yet done, saying, My counsel shall stand, and I will do all my pleasure:
[11] Calling a ravenous bird from the east, the man that executeth my counsel from a far country: yea, I have spoken it, I will also bring it to pass; I have purposed it, I will also do it.

Lean Not

Proverbs 3:5-6; James 1:5 (KJV)

Proverbs 3:5-6 (KJV)
5 Trust in the Lord with all thine heart; and lean not unto thine own understanding.
6 In all thy ways acknowledge him, and he shall direct thy paths.

James 1:5 (KJV)
5 If any of you lack wisdom, let him ask of God, that giveth to all men liberally, and upbraideth not; and it shall be given him.

Love is An Action

Philippians 4:19 (KJV)

Philippians 4:19 (KJV)
[19] But my God shall supply all your need according to his riches in glory by Christ Jesus.

Chapter 5 – Fighting the Enemy

But for Your Praying Saints 143
Idols, Idols, Idols 144
It's War! 145
Just Do It! 146
The Perfect Murder 147
Put it All On! 148
What's His Face? 149

Dr. Lydia A. Woods

But for Your Praying Saints

Ephesians 6:18; 1 Thessalonians 5:17; James 5:16 (KJV)

Ephesians 6:18 (KJV)
[18] Praying always with all prayer and supplication in the Spirit, and watching thereunto with all perseverance and supplication for all saints;

1 Thessalonians 5:17 (KJV)
[17] Pray without ceasing.

James 5:16 (KJV)
[16] Confess your faults one to another, and pray one for another, that ye may be healed. The effectual fervent prayer of a righteous man availeth much.

Idols, Idols, Idols

1 John 5:21 (KJV)

1 John 5:21 (KJV)
21 Little children, keep yourselves from idols. Amen.

Dr. Lydia A. Woods

It's War!

Ephesians 6:10-17 (KJV)

Ephesians 6:10-17 (KJV)
[10] Finally, my brethren, be strong in the Lord, and in the power of his might.
[11] Put on the whole armour of God, that ye may be able to stand against the wiles of the devil.
[12] For we wrestle not against flesh and blood, but against principalities, against powers, against the rulers of the darkness of this world, against spiritual wickedness in high places.
[13] Wherefore take unto you the whole armour of God, that ye may be able to withstand in the evil day, and having done all, to stand.
[14] Stand therefore, having your loins girt about with truth, and having on the breastplate of righteousness;
[15] And your feet shod with the preparation of the gospel of peace;
[16] Above all, taking the shield of faith, wherewith ye shall be able to quench all the fiery darts of the wicked.
[17] And take the helmet of salvation, and the sword of the Spirit, which is the word of God:

Just Do It!

Mark 16:15-20 (KJV)

Mark 16:15-20 (KJV)

[15] And he said unto them, Go ye into all the world, and preach the gospel to every creature.

[16] He that believeth and is baptized shall be saved; but he that believeth not shall be damned.

[17] And these signs shall follow them that believe; In my name shall they cast out devils; they shall speak with new tongues;

[18] They shall take up serpents; and if they drink any deadly thing, it shall not hurt them; they shall lay hands on the sick, and they shall recover.

[19] So then after the Lord had spoken unto them, he was received up into heaven, and sat on the right hand of God.

[20] And they went forth, and preached every where, the Lord working with them, and confirming the word with signs following. Amen.

Dr. Lydia A. Woods

The Perfect Murder

Romans 7:14-21 (KJV)

Romans 7:14-21 (KJV)
[14] For we know that the law is spiritual: but I am carnal, sold under sin.
[15] For that which I do I allow not: for what I would, that do I not; but what I hate, that do I.
[16] If then I do that which I would not, I consent unto the law that it is good.
[17] Now then it is no more I that do it, but sin that dwelleth in me.
[18] For I know that in me (that is, in my flesh,) dwelleth no good thing: for to will is present with me; but how to perform that which is good I find not.
[19] For the good that I would I do not: but the evil which I would not, that I do.
[20] Now if I do that I would not, it is no more I that do it, but sin that dwelleth in me.
[21] I find then a law, that, when I would do good, evil is present with me.

Put it All On!

Ephesians 6:11-17 (KJV)

Ephesians 6:11-17 (KJV)

11 Put on the whole armour of God, that ye may be able to stand against the wiles of the devil.

12 For we wrestle not against flesh and blood, but against principalities, against powers, against the rulers of the darkness of this world, against spiritual wickedness in high places.

13 Wherefore take unto you the whole armour of God, that ye may be able to withstand in the evil day, and having done all, to stand.

14 Stand therefore, having your loins girt about with truth, and having on the breastplate of righteousness;

15 And your feet shod with the preparation of the gospel of peace;

16 Above all, taking the shield of faith, wherewith ye shall be able to quench all the fiery darts of the wicked.

17 And take the helmet of salvation, and the sword of the Spirit, which is the word of God:

Dr. Lydia A. Woods

What's His Face?

Genesis 3:15; John 19:11 (KJV)

Genesis 3:15 (KJV)
15 And I will put enmity between thee and the woman, and between thy seed and her seed; it shall bruise thy head, and thou shalt bruise his heel.

John 19:11 (KJV)
11 Jesus answered, Thou couldest have no power at all against me, except it were given thee from above: therefore he that delivered me unto thee hath the greater sin.

Chapter 6 – Those Bible People

Follow the Anointing 151
Here I Am 153
Highly Favored 155
Joseph 156
Just Said No 158
She Was First 159
So Be Like Job 163

Dr. Lydia A. Woods

Follow the Anointing

1 Samuel 18:1-4, 20:14-17; 2 Samuel 1:11-12, 17, 25-27 (KJV)

1 Samuel 18:1-4 (KJV)

[1] And it came to pass, when he had made an end of speaking unto Saul, that the soul of Jonathan was knit with the soul of David, and Jonathan loved him as his own soul.

[2] And Saul took him that day, and would let him go no more home to his father's house.

[3] Then Jonathan and David made a covenant, because he loved him as his own soul.

[4] And Jonathan stripped himself of the robe that was upon him, and gave it to David, and his garments, even to his sword, and to his bow, and to his girdle.

1 Samuel 20:14-17 (KJV)

[14] And thou shalt not only while yet I live shew me the kindness of the Lord, that I die not:

[15] But also thou shalt not cut off thy kindness from my house for ever: no, not when the Lord hath cut off the enemies of David every one from the face of the earth.

[16] So Jonathan made a covenant with the house of David, saying, Let the Lord even require it at the hand of David's enemies.

[17] And Jonathan caused David to swear again, because he loved him: for he loved him as he loved his own soul.

2 Samuel 1:11-12 (KJV)

[11] Then David took hold on his clothes, and rent them; and likewise all the men that were with him:

[12] And they mourned, and wept, and fasted until even, for Saul, and for Jonathan his son, and for the people of the Lord, and for the house of Israel; because they were fallen by the sword.

2 Samuel 1:17 (KJV)

[17] And David lamented with this lamentation over Saul and over Jonathan his son:

2 Samuel 1:25-27 (KJV)
[25] How are the mighty fallen in the midst of the battle! O Jonathan, thou wast slain in thine high places.
[26] I am distressed for thee, my brother Jonathan: very pleasant hast thou been unto me: thy love to me was wonderful, passing the love of women.
[27] How are the mighty fallen, and the weapons of war perished!

Dr. Lydia A. Woods

Here I Am

1 Samuel 3 (KJV)

1 Samuel 3 (KJV)
[1] And the child Samuel ministered unto the Lord before Eli. And the word of the Lord was precious in those days; there was no open vision.
[2] And it came to pass at that time, when Eli was laid down in his place, and his eyes began to wax dim, that he could not see;
[3] And ere the lamp of God went out in the temple of the Lord, where the ark of God was, and Samuel was laid down to sleep;
[4] That the Lord called Samuel: and he answered, Here am I.
[5] And he ran unto Eli, and said, Here am I; for thou calledst me. And he said, I called not; lie down again. And he went and lay down.
[6] And the Lord called yet again, Samuel. And Samuel arose and went to Eli, and said, Here am I; for thou didst call me. And he answered, I called not, my son; lie down again.
[7] Now Samuel did not yet know the Lord, neither was the word of the Lord yet revealed unto him.
[8] And the Lord called Samuel again the third time. And he arose and went to Eli, and said, Here am I; for thou didst call me. And Eli perceived that the Lord had called the child.
[9] Therefore Eli said unto Samuel, Go, lie down: and it shall be, if he call thee, that thou shalt say, Speak, Lord; for thy servant heareth. So Samuel went and lay down in his place.
[10] And the Lord came, and stood, and called as at other times, Samuel, Samuel. Then Samuel answered, Speak; for thy servant heareth.
[11] And the Lord said to Samuel, Behold, I will do a thing in Israel, at which both the ears of every one that heareth it shall tingle.
[12] In that day I will perform against Eli all things which I have spoken concerning his house: when I begin, I will also make an end.

¹³ For I have told him that I will judge his house for ever for the iniquity which he knoweth; because his sons made themselves vile, and he restrained them not.
¹⁴ And therefore I have sworn unto the house of Eli, that the iniquity of Eli's house shall not be purged with sacrifice nor offering for ever.
¹⁵ And Samuel lay until the morning, and opened the doors of the house of the Lord. And Samuel feared to shew Eli the vision.
¹⁶ Then Eli called Samuel, and said, Samuel, my son. And he answered, Here am I.
¹⁷ And he said, What is the thing that the Lord hath said unto thee? I pray thee hide it not from me: God do so to thee, and more also, if thou hide any thing from me of all the things that he said unto thee.
¹⁸ And Samuel told him every whit, and hid nothing from him. And he said, It is the Lord: let him do what seemeth him good.
¹⁹ And Samuel grew, and the Lord was with him, and did let none of his words fall to the ground.
²⁰ And all Israel from Dan even to Beersheba knew that Samuel was established to be a prophet of the Lord.
²¹ And the Lord appeared again in Shiloh: for the Lord revealed himself to Samuel in Shiloh by the word of the Lord.

Dr. Lydia A. Woods

Highly Favored

Luke 1:27-38 (KJV)

Luke 1:27-38 (KJV)
27 To a virgin espoused to a man whose name was Joseph, of the house of David; and the virgin's name was Mary.
28 And the angel came in unto her, and said, Hail, thou that art highly favoured, the Lord is with thee: blessed art thou among women.
29 And when she saw him, she was troubled at his saying, and cast in her mind what manner of salutation this should be.
30 And the angel said unto her, Fear not, Mary: for thou hast found favour with God.
31 And, behold, thou shalt conceive in thy womb, and bring forth a son, and shalt call his name Jesus.
32 He shall be great, and shall be called the Son of the Highest: and the Lord God shall give unto him the throne of his father David:
33 And he shall reign over the house of Jacob for ever; and of his kingdom there shall be no end.
34 Then said Mary unto the angel, How shall this be, seeing I know not a man?
35 And the angel answered and said unto her, The Holy Ghost shall come upon thee, and the power of the Highest shall overshadow thee: therefore also that holy thing which shall be born of thee shall be called the Son of God.
36 And, behold, thy cousin Elisabeth, she hath also conceived a son in her old age: and this is the sixth month with her, who was called barren.
37 For with God nothing shall be impossible.
38 And Mary said, Behold the handmaid of the Lord; be it unto me according to thy word. And the angel departed from her.

Joseph

Genesis 37:2-5, 9, 15; 31-35; 41:41-43; 45:1-5 (KJV)

Genesis 37:2-5 (KJV)

² These are the generations of Jacob. Joseph, being seventeen years old, was feeding the flock with his brethren; and the lad was with the sons of Bilhah, and with the sons of Zilpah, his father's wives: and Joseph brought unto his father their evil report.

³ Now Israel loved Joseph more than all his children, because he was the son of his old age: and he made him a coat of many colours.

⁴ And when his brethren saw that their father loved him more than all his brethren, they hated him, and could not speak peaceably unto him.

⁵ And Joseph dreamed a dream, and he told it his brethren: and they hated him yet the more.

Genesis 37:9 (KJV)

⁹ And he dreamed yet another dream, and told it his brethren, and said, Behold, I have dreamed a dream more; and, behold, the sun and the moon and the eleven stars made obeisance to me.

Genesis 37:15 (KJV)

¹⁵ And a certain man found him, and, behold, he was wandering in the field: and the man asked him, saying, What seekest thou?

Genesis 37:31-35 (KJV)

³¹ And they took Joseph's coat, and killed a kid of the goats, and dipped the coat in the blood;

³² And they sent the coat of many colours, and they brought it to their father; and said, This have we found: know now whether it be thy son's coat or no.

³³ And he knew it, and said, It is my son's coat; an evil beast hath devoured him; Joseph is without doubt rent in pieces.

³⁴ And Jacob rent his clothes, and put sackcloth upon his loins, and mourned for his son many days.

35 And all his sons and all his daughters rose up to comfort him; but he refused to be comforted; and he said, For I will go down into the grave unto my son mourning. Thus his father wept for him.

Genesis 41:41-43 (KJV)
41 And Pharaoh said unto Joseph, See, I have set thee over all the land of Egypt.
42 And Pharaoh took off his ring from his hand, and put it upon Joseph's hand, and arrayed him in vestures of fine linen, and put a gold chain about his neck;
43 And he made him to ride in the second chariot which he had; and they cried before him, Bow the knee: and he made him ruler over all the land of Egypt.

Genesis 45:1-5 (KJV)
1 Then Joseph could not refrain himself before all them that stood by him; and he cried, Cause every man to go out from me. And there stood no man with him, while Joseph made himself known unto his brethren.
2 And he wept aloud: and the Egyptians and the house of Pharaoh heard.
3 And Joseph said unto his brethren, I am Joseph; doth my father yet live? And his brethren could not answer him; for they were troubled at his presence.
4 And Joseph said unto his brethren, Come near to me, I pray you. And they came near. And he said, I am Joseph your brother, whom ye sold into Egypt.
5 Now therefore be not grieved, nor angry with yourselves, that ye sold me hither: for God did send me before you to preserve life.

Just Said No

Daniel 3:1-6 (KJV)

Daniel 3:1-6 (KJV)

¹ Nebuchadnezzar the king made an image of gold, whose height was threescore cubits, and the breadth thereof six cubits: he set it up in the plain of Dura, in the province of Babylon.

² Then Nebuchadnezzar the king sent to gather together the princes, the governors, and the captains, the judges, the treasurers, the counsellors, the sheriffs, and all the rulers of the provinces, to come to the dedication of the image which Nebuchadnezzar the king had set up.

³ Then the princes, the governors, and captains, the judges, the treasurers, the counsellors, the sheriffs, and all the rulers of the provinces, were gathered together unto the dedication of the image that Nebuchadnezzar the king had set up; and they stood before the image that Nebuchadnezzar had set up.

⁴ Then an herald cried aloud, To you it is commanded, O people, nations, and languages,

⁵ That at what time ye hear the sound of the cornet, flute, harp, sackbut, psaltery, dulcimer, and all kinds of musick, ye fall down and worship the golden image that Nebuchadnezzar the king hath set up:

⁶ And whoso falleth not down and worshippeth shall the same hour be cast into the midst of a burning fiery furnace.

Dr. Lydia A. Woods

She Was First

John 20:1-18; Luke 24:1-10; Mark 16:1-11; Matthew 28:1-8 (KJV)

John 20:1-18 (KJV)

[1] The first day of the week cometh Mary Magdalene early, when it was yet dark, unto the sepulchre, and seeth the stone taken away from the sepulchre.

[2] Then she runneth, and cometh to Simon Peter, and to the other disciple, whom Jesus loved, and saith unto them, They have taken away the Lord out of the sepulchre, and we know not where they have laid him.

[3] Peter therefore went forth, and that other disciple, and came to the sepulchre.

[4] So they ran both together: and the other disciple did outrun Peter, and came first to the sepulchre.

[5] And he stooping down, and looking in, saw the linen clothes lying; yet went he not in.

[6] Then cometh Simon Peter following him, and went into the sepulchre, and seeth the linen clothes lie,

[7] And the napkin, that was about his head, not lying with the linen clothes, but wrapped together in a place by itself.

[8] Then went in also that other disciple, which came first to the sepulchre, and he saw, and believed.

[9] For as yet they knew not the scripture, that he must rise again from the dead.

[10] Then the disciples went away again unto their own home.

[11] But Mary stood without at the sepulchre weeping: and as she wept, she stooped down, and looked into the sepulchre,

[12] And seeth two angels in white sitting, the one at the head, and the other at the feet, where the body of Jesus had lain.

[13] And they say unto her, Woman, why weepest thou? She saith unto them, Because they have taken away my Lord, and I know not where they have laid him.

¹⁴ And when she had thus said, she turned herself back, and saw Jesus standing, and knew not that it was Jesus.
¹⁵ Jesus saith unto her, Woman, why weepest thou? whom seekest thou? She, supposing him to be the gardener, saith unto him, Sir, if thou have borne him hence, tell me where thou hast laid him, and I will take him away.
¹⁶ Jesus saith unto her, Mary. She turned herself, and saith unto him, Rabboni; which is to say, Master.
¹⁷ Jesus saith unto her, Touch me not; for I am not yet ascended to my Father: but go to my brethren, and say unto them, I ascend unto my Father, and your Father; and to my God, and your God.
¹⁸ Mary Magdalene came and told the disciples that she had seen the Lord, and that he had spoken these things unto her.

Luke 24:1-10 (KJV)
¹ Now upon the first day of the week, very early in the morning, they came unto the sepulchre, bringing the spices which they had prepared, and certain others with them.
² And they found the stone rolled away from the sepulchre.
³ And they entered in, and found not the body of the Lord Jesus.
⁴ And it came to pass, as they were much perplexed thereabout, behold, two men stood by them in shining garments:
⁵ And as they were afraid, and bowed down their faces to the earth, they said unto them, Why seek ye the living among the dead?
⁶ He is not here, but is risen: remember how he spake unto you when he was yet in Galilee,
⁷ Saying, The Son of man must be delivered into the hands of sinful men, and be crucified, and the third day rise again.
⁸ And they remembered his words,

⁹ And returned from the sepulchre, and told all these things unto the eleven, and to all the rest.

¹⁰ It was Mary Magdalene and Joanna, and Mary the mother of James, and other women that were with them, which told these things unto the apostles.

Mark 16:1-11 (KJV)
¹ And when the sabbath was past, Mary Magdalene, and Mary the mother of James, and Salome, had bought sweet spices, that they might come and anoint him.

² And very early in the morning the first day of the week, they came unto the sepulchre at the rising of the sun.

³ And they said among themselves, Who shall roll us away the stone from the door of the sepulchre?

⁴ And when they looked, they saw that the stone was rolled away: for it was very great.

⁵ And entering into the sepulchre, they saw a young man sitting on the right side, clothed in a long white garment; and they were affrighted.

⁶ And he saith unto them, Be not affrighted: Ye seek Jesus of Nazareth, which was crucified: he is risen; he is not here: behold the place where they laid him.

⁷ But go your way, tell his disciples and Peter that he goeth before you into Galilee: there shall ye see him, as he said unto you.

⁸ And they went out quickly, and fled from the sepulchre; for they trembled and were amazed: neither said they any thing to any man; for they were afraid.

⁹ Now when Jesus was risen early the first day of the week, he appeared first to Mary Magdalene, out of whom he had cast seven devils.

¹⁰ And she went and told them that had been with him, as they mourned and wept.

¹¹ And they, when they had heard that he was alive, and had been seen of her, believed not.

Matthew 28:1-8 (KJV)
¹ In the end of the sabbath, as it began to dawn toward the first day of the week, came Mary Magdalene and the other Mary to see the sepulchre.

² And, behold, there was a great earthquake: for the angel of the Lord descended from heaven, and came and rolled back the stone from the door, and sat upon it.

³ His countenance was like lightning, and his raiment white as snow:

⁴ And for fear of him the keepers did shake, and became as dead men.

⁵ And the angel answered and said unto the women, Fear not ye: for I know that ye seek Jesus, which was crucified.

⁶ He is not here: for he is risen, as he said. Come, see the place where the Lord lay.

⁷ And go quickly, and tell his disciples that he is risen from the dead; and, behold, he goeth before you into Galilee; there shall ye see him: lo, I have told you.

⁸ And they departed quickly from the sepulchre with fear and great joy; and did run to bring his disciples word.

Dr. Lydia A. Woods

So Be Like Job

Job 1:1, 8-12; 2:1-6; 42:12-13 (KJV)

Job 1:1 (KJV)
[1] There was a man in the land of Uz, whose name was Job; and that man was perfect and upright, and one that feared God, and eschewed evil.

Job 1:8-12 (KJV)
[8] And the Lord said unto Satan, Hast thou considered my servant Job, that there is none like him in the earth, a perfect and an upright man, one that feareth God, and escheweth evil?
[9] Then Satan answered the Lord, and said, Doth Job fear God for nought?
[10] Hast not thou made an hedge about him, and about his house, and about all that he hath on every side? thou hast blessed the work of his hands, and his substance is increased in the land.
[11] But put forth thine hand now, and touch all that he hath, and he will curse thee to thy face.
[12] And the Lord said unto Satan, Behold, all that he hath is in thy power; only upon himself put not forth thine hand. So Satan went forth from the presence of the Lord.

Job 2:1-6 (KJV)
[1] Again there was a day when the sons of God came to present themselves before the Lord, and Satan came also among them to present himself before the Lord.
[2] And the Lord said unto Satan, From whence comest thou? And Satan answered the Lord, and said, From going to and fro in the earth, and from walking up and down in it.

³ And the Lord said unto Satan, Hast thou considered my servant Job, that there is none like him in the earth, a perfect and an upright man, one that feareth God, and escheweth evil? and still he holdeth fast his integrity, although thou movedst me against him, to destroy him without cause.
⁴ And Satan answered the Lord, and said, Skin for skin, yea, all that a man hath will he give for his life.
⁵ But put forth thine hand now, and touch his bone and his flesh, and he will curse thee to thy face.
⁶ And the Lord said unto Satan, Behold, he is in thine hand; but save his life.

Job 42:12-13 (KJV)
¹² So the Lord blessed the latter end of Job more than his beginning: for he had fourteen thousand sheep, and six thousand camels, and a thousand yoke of oxen, and a thousand she asses.
¹³ He had also seven sons and three daughters.

Chapter 7 –
The Movies:
Their Spiritual Messages

The Circle of Life 166
E.T. 168
If You Build It 169
May the Force 170
The Mummy's Curse 171
The Red Pill or the Blue 172
The Richest Man in Town 173

The Circle of Life

Genesis 4:1-11; 33:4,10-11 (KJV)

Genesis 4:1-11 (KJV)

[1] And Adam knew Eve his wife; and she conceived, and bare Cain, and said, I have gotten a man from the Lord.

[2] And she again bare his brother Abel. And Abel was a keeper of sheep, but Cain was a tiller of the ground.

[3] And in process of time it came to pass, that Cain brought of the fruit of the ground an offering unto the Lord.

[4] And Abel, he also brought of the firstlings of his flock and of the fat thereof. And the Lord had respect unto Abel and to his offering:

[5] But unto Cain and to his offering he had not respect. And Cain was very wroth, and his countenance fell.

[6] And the Lord said unto Cain, Why art thou wroth? and why is thy countenance fallen?

[7] If thou doest well, shalt thou not be accepted? and if thou doest not well, sin lieth at the door. And unto thee shall be his desire, and thou shalt rule over him.

[8] And Cain talked with Abel his brother: and it came to pass, when they were in the field, that Cain rose up against Abel his brother, and slew him.

[9] And the Lord said unto Cain, Where is Abel thy brother? And he said, I know not: Am I my brother's keeper?

[10] And he said, What hast thou done? the voice of thy brother's blood crieth unto me from the ground.

[11] And now art thou cursed from the earth, which hath opened her mouth to receive thy brother's blood from thy hand;

Genesis 33:4 (KJV)

[4] And Esau ran to meet him, and embraced him, and fell on his neck, and kissed him: and they wept.

Genesis 33:10-11 (KJV)

[10] And Jacob said, Nay, I pray thee, if now I have found grace in thy sight, then receive my present at my hand: for therefore I have seen thy face, as though I had seen the face of God, and thou wast pleased with me.
[11] Take, I pray thee, my blessing that is brought to thee; because God hath dealt graciously with me, and because I have enough. And he urged him, and he took it.

E.T.

John 14:1-4 (KJV)

John 14:1-4 (KJV)
¹ Let not your heart be troubled: ye believe in God, believe also in me.
² In my Father's house are many mansions: if it were not so, I would have told you. I go to prepare a place for you.
³ And if I go and prepare a place for you, I will come again, and receive you unto myself; that where I am, there ye may be also.
⁴ And whither I go ye know, and the way ye know.

Dr. Lydia A. Woods

If You Build It

1 Samuel 15:22; Hebrews 11:6; John 10:27; Philippians 2:13; Ephesians 1:9 (KJV)

1 Samuel 15:22 (KJV)
22 And Samuel said, Hath the Lord as great delight in burnt offerings and sacrifices, as in obeying the voice of the Lord? Behold, to obey is better than sacrifice, and to hearken than the fat of rams.

Hebrews 11:6 (KJV)
6 But without faith it is impossible to please him: for he that cometh to God must believe that he is, and that he is a rewarder of them that diligently seek him.

John 10:27 (KJV)
27 My sheep hear my voice, and I know them, and they follow me:

Philippians 2:13 (KJV)
13 For it is God which worketh in you both to will and to do of his good pleasure.

Ephesians 1:9 (KJV)
9 Having made known unto us the mystery of his will, according to his good pleasure which he hath purposed in himself:

May the Force...

1 Corinthians 13:4-7 (KJV)

1 Corinthians 13:4-7 (KJV)
⁴ Charity suffereth long, and is kind; charity envieth not; charity vaunteth not itself, is not puffed up,
⁵ Doth not behave itself unseemly, seeketh not her own, is not easily provoked, thinketh no evil;
⁶ Rejoiceth not in iniquity, but rejoiceth in the truth;
⁷ Beareth all things, believeth all things, hopeth all things, endureth all things.

Dr. Lydia A. Woods

The Mummy's Curse

Romans 6:6-7 (KJV)

Romans 6:6-7 (KJV)
⁶ Knowing this, that our old man is crucified with him, that the body of sin might be destroyed, that henceforth we should not serve sin. ⁷ For he that is dead is freed from sin.

The Red Pill or the Blue

John 10:10; Romans 12:2-3; Proverbs 9:10 (KJV)

John 10:10 (KJV)
[10] The thief cometh not, but for to steal, and to kill, and to destroy: I am come that they might have life, and that they might have it more abundantly.

Romans 12:2-3 (KJV)
[2] And be not conformed to this world: but be ye transformed by the renewing of your mind, that ye may prove what is that good, and acceptable, and perfect, will of God.
[3] For I say, through the grace given unto me, to every man that is among you, not to think of himself more highly than he ought to think; but to think soberly, according as God hath dealt to every man the measure of faith.

Proverbs 9:10 (KJV)
[10] The fear of the Lord is the beginning of wisdom: and the knowledge of the holy is understanding.

Dr. Lydia A. Woods

The Richest Man in Town

John 15:13; Matthew 6:19; Proverbs 18:22; Psalms 91:11 (KJV)

John 15:13 (KJV)
13 Greater love hath no man than this, that a man lay down his life for his friends.

Matthew 6:19 (KJV)
19 Lay not up for yourselves treasures upon earth, where moth and rust doth corrupt, and where thieves break through and steal:

Proverbs 18:22 (KJV)
22 Whoso findeth a wife findeth a good thing, and obtaineth favour of the Lord.

Psalms 91:11 (KJV)
11 For he shall give his angels charge over thee, to keep thee in all thy ways.

Scriptural Index

Genesis
1:3
  He's Good At, 103
1:9
  He's Good At, 103
1:12
  He's Good At, 103
1:16
  He's Good At, 103
1:24
  He's Good At, 103
1:27
  He's Good At, 103
1:31
  He's Good At, 103
3:15
  What's His Face?, 149
4:1-11
  The Circle of Life, 166
12:3
  I'm Not Lucky – I'm Blessed, 118
33:4
  The Circle of Life, 166
33:10-11
  The Circle of Life, 166
37:2-5
  Joseph, 156
37:9
  Joseph, 156
37:15
  Joseph, 156
37:31-35
  Joseph, 156
41:41-43
  Joseph, 156
45:1-5
  Joseph, 156

Exodus
11:2
  Doin' the Israelite, 135
13:21
  Doin' the Israelite, 135
14:27-28
  Doin' the Israelite, 135
16:2-3
  Doin' the Israelite, 135
16:12
  Doin' the Israelite, 135
17:2-4
  Doin' the Israelite, 135

Deuteronomy
7:3-14
  I'm Not Lucky – I'm Blessed, 118

1 Samuel
3
  Here I Am, 153
15:22
  If You Build It, 169
18:1-4
  Follow the Anointing, 151
20:14-17
  Follow the Anointing, 151

2 Samuel
1:11-12
  Follow the Anointing, 151
1:17
  Follow the Anointing, 151
1:25-27
  Follow the Anointing, 151

2 Chronicles
30:8
  Back Talk, 134

Job
1:1
  So Be Like Job, 163

1:8-12
   So Be Like Job, 163
2:1-6
   So Be Like Job, 163
33:6
   Your Gifts and Talents, 132
42:12-13
   So Be Like Job, 163

Psalms
31:19
   Simply Because You Are Mine, 122
46:10
   Be Still!, 125
95:7
   That Small Still Voice, 110
139:1-6
   It is Your Destiny, 120
139:14-18
   It is Your Destiny, 120

Proverbs
3:1-18
   Happy is the Woman or Man, 128
3:5-6
   Lean Not, 140
9:10
   The Red Pill or the Blue, 172
19:21
   If You Want To Make God Laugh!, 139

Isaiah
14:27
   He's Good At, 103

29:16
   Your Gifts and Talents, 132
45:9
   Your Gifts and Talents, 132
46:9-11
   He's Good At, 103
   If You Want To Make God Laugh!, 139
64:4
   Simply Because You Are Mine, 122
64:8
   Your Gifts and Talents, 132

Daniel
3:1-6
   Just Said No, 158

Hosea
2:19
   With His Own Blood, 111

Matthew
4:1
   Master of Masters, 105
4:19
   Master of Masters, 105
5:1
   Master of Masters, 105
5:14-16
   The Brightest Light, 116
5:36
   If You Want To Make God Laugh!, 139
6:10
   Your Gifts and Talents, 132

7:11
  Simply Because You Are Mine, 122
7:29
  Master of Masters, 105
8:26
  Master of Masters, 105
11:5
  Master of Masters, 105
21:24
  A Bible Character, 113
25:45
  Your Gifts and Talents, 132
28:1-8
  She Was First, 159
Mark
5:35-43
  Be Not Afraid, Only Believe, 124
11:25-26
  Forgive or Forgive Not, 137
15:1
  A Bible Character, 113
13:24-27
  Good News, 126
15:10-11
  A Bible Character, 113
16:1
  A Bible Character, 113
16:1-11
  She Was First, 159
16:15-20
  Just Do It!, 146
Luke
1:27-28
  Highly Favored, 155

2:26
  Somethin' Told Me, 109
4:1-13
  If Thou Be..., 117
6:37
  Forgive or Forgive Not, 137
8:43-48
  Master of Masters, 105
17:21
  Scariest Journey, 121
22:47
  A Bible Character, 113
22:57
  A Bible Character, 113
22:60
  A Bible Character, 113
23:21-34
  A Bible Character, 113
24:1-10
  She Was First, 159
John
1:1-5
  Ain't He All That!, 102
2:1-11
  Master of Masters, 105
10:10
  The Red Pill or the Blue, 172
10:27
  If You Build It, 169
11:43-44
  Master of Masters, 105
12:26
  Somethin' Told Me, 109
14:1-4
  E.T., 168

Scriptural Index

14:6
  Scariest Journey, 121
15:13
  Hero in You, 130
19:11
  What's His Face?, 149
20:1-18
  She Was First, 159
Acts
20:28
  With His Own Blood, 111
Romans
6:6-7
  The Mummy's Curse, 171
7:14-21
  The Perfect Murder, 147
12:2-3
  The Red Pill or the Blue, 172
12:3
  Pieces of Myself, 108
1 Corinthians
2:9-11
  Simply Because You Are Mine, 122
13:4-7
  May the Force…, 170
15:3
  Good News, 126
15:52
  Good News, 126
Ephesians
1:9
  If You Build It, 169
2:2
  Back Talk, 134

4:7
  Pieces of Myself, 108
4:30
  Somethin' Told Me, 109
6:10-17
  It's War!, 145
6:11-17
  Put it All On!, 148
6:18
  But for Your Praying Saints, 143
Philippians
2:13
  If You Build It, 169
4:8-9
  Garbage in Garbage Out!, 138
4:19
  Love is An Action, 141
1 Thessalonians
5:17
  But for Your Praying Saints, 143
Hebrews
1:2-3
  Ain't He All That!, 102
3:7
  That Small Still Voice, 110
11:6
  If You Build It, 169
13:5
  Pieces of Myself, 108
James
1:5
  It's Alright, 131
  Lean Not, 140

5:16
   But for Your Praying Saints, 143
1 Peter
  1:2
   Back Talk, 134
  2:9
   A Bible Character, 113
1 John
  5:21
   Idols, Idols, Idols, 144
Revelation
  1:7
   Good News, 126

19:7-9
   Good News, 126
   With His Own Blood, 111
20:1-3
   Good News, 126
21:1-5
   Good News, 126
21:9
   With His Own Blood, 111
22:13
   Ain't He All That!, 102

www.ingramcontent.com/pod-product-compliance
Lightning Source LLC
Chambersburg PA
CBHW071500040426
42444CB00008B/1424